Journey Out of Darkness

Journey Out of Darkness

by MARIE BELL McCOY

DAVID McKAY COMPANY, INC.

New York

JOURNEY OUT OF DARKNESS

COPYRIGHT © 1963 BY MARIE BELL MC COY

Second Printing December 1964

LIBRARY OF CONGRESS CATALOG CARD NUMBER: 63-19346

MANUFACTURED IN THE UNITED STATES OF AMERICA

VAN REES PRESS • NEW YORK

For my husband

CLYDE McCOY

who has come the long journey with me
and whose eyes have been my eyes
every step of the way

Foreword

Journey Out of Darkness has been written out of gratitude that I was given courage and perseverance on my journey from the gloomy canyon of despair, incident to sudden blindness, up into the luminous high country of fulfillment and peace which I now enjoy.

It has been written, too, in the hope that others, through my experience, may be encouraged to seek a "road out" of their own difficulties. My problem has been blindness but this book is not a biography of that blindness—the blindness was but the catapult that sent me into a new area of understanding and endeavor. The trail of my effort is plain and can be picked up by persons dealing with widely differing problems—physical or emotional—of any kind or degree.

To read here of an average woman's mastery over self and a tragic problem will, I believe, encourage the reader to say—If she could do it, why can't I?

The answer is simple. You can. The whole matter is one of choice. You may choose to go limp under your particular burden, retire to a chimney corner or some equally sooty spot and eke out the rest of your days whimpering and sniveling, a reproach to yourself and a nuisance to those you should hold dear. Or, you can regard your problem as a resplendent and irresistible challenge—a challenge to achieve your potential stature.

I pray that you choose the latter and that God will grant you —as He granted me—His grace, His strength, and a sizable sense of humor.

MARIE BELL McCOY

JUNE 4, 1963

Contents

Journey Out of Darkness

CHAPTER 1

My Sighted Life

SOMETIMES I wonder if the kind of life I lived in my sighted days has made adjustment to blindness more difficult for me or whether that previous life, by its very nature, eases my present existence as a blind woman—makes it more tolerable.

For my life as a sighted person was filled with visual enjoyment and today I deeply, sorely, miss that life. Paradoxically, the very thing which I miss most is what now supports me in great measure. For in all those years of sight I responded with ardor to what my eyes showed me and these things, recorded in my memory, built up the storehouse on which I draw heavily today.

When misfortune, in the guise of blindness, knocked on our door—and I say "our" because my husband, Clyde, heard that

1

sharp rap with as heavy a heart as mine—our life was a pleasant one indeed, full of activity, of interests developed over the years —a life which, like that of most persons, had had its quota of perplexities and disappointments but which, over all, had been a happy one.

We had been living in New York City for more than twenty-five years and, although neither of us was native to it, we had grown to feel that we were a part of the great metropolis. My husband's connection with a large chain of hotels provided more than comfortably for us and the easy way of life which a good hotel always affords freed me from all domestic responsibility. Thus the daytime was my own—to do with as I pleased—but the evenings, when Clyde was usually free of duties, we spent together. We were generally in accord about the choice for our evening's activity. In fact, one of the great happinesses of our life together stems from our exceptional congeniality of tastes. This has enabled us to enjoy together whatever life has offered. Marriage is always a gamble and the stakes are high, being, in fact, two human lives. We are among those lucky ones whose marriage has endured over a goodly span of years. It is our great good fortune to have a similar sense of humor—something we believe to be a basic ingredient for a happy, lasting marriage. Shared experience is another amalgam. Together we have welded many fine friendships, have traveled widely together, and together have faced many crucial situations—financial, personal, and the ultimate, the death of our only child.

New York is, literally, all things to all men. The occasional visitor to the city comes with a yard-long list of Things-To-Do and a comparatively short time in which to do them. The result is something stuffed tighter than a sausage. On the other hand, resident New Yorkers have a comfortable cushion of time in which to avail themselves of what the city offers.

Clyde and I had a lively interest in many things, a tolerant interest in many others. Wherever possible we avoided boredom. If we liked to do a thing, we did it but if we disliked doing it we let it alone, no matter how much it might take the fancy of others. From the earliest days of our marriage we had endeavored to establish what we were willing to spend our time and money on and, conversely, what we were unwilling to spend our time and money on. Experience has taught us how important the latter is.

Together, then, we enjoyed the wide range of the New York theater, the Symphony, the recitals of many great artists. Seldom did we attend the Opera together for the simple reason that my husband's interest in this art form is wan, feeble. I myself was an inveterate opera-goer. On my opera nights Clyde would elect to go to some sports event at Madison Square Garden. This arrangement gave us both a fine evening. Like most people we enjoyed dining out, not only in many and varied restaurants in the city but also in the homes of friends.

Countless evenings we spent quietly in our apartment, reading or listening to recordings. We rarely read aloud to each other for Clyde likes to read rapidly while it was my wont to read slowly, rereading a phrase or paragraph again and again, savoring its style as well as its content. We read many books, a variety of magazines and, unfailingly, two large metropolitan dailies—whose contents provide a feast for the alert, inquiring mind, the teachable mind. These hours were quiet ones, during which I always felt the reservoir of my whole self was being replenished.

Some of our finest evenings were spent at ballet performances, for the ballet had become an enthusiasm with both of us. Here

3

was music, color, form, rhythm, pattern, meaning—all rolled into one great rich "strudel." Today my delight would know no bounds if I might have even a few crumbs from such a strudel.

Life was even more pleasant after we bought a house with a small acreage in Dutchess County where we could go for rest and diversion on week ends and holidays. We called it "MARCLY"—a word coined years before from the first letters of our names and always given to our vacation houses—Marcly Lodge, Marcly Cottage, Marcly Landing. It is unlikely we shall ever have anything so lordly as Marcly Manor.

Like many city dwellers, Clyde for years had had his dream of a country garden. Every spring I watched him as, with more and better tools and fertilizers, he would start afresh. Every year the effort ended in defeat. We grew to have an enormous respect for the wit and persistence of wild creatures. No matter how high we built the garden fence, deer jumped it and nibbled tidbits. No matter how deep down we set it, the woodchucks burrowed deeper. The brazen birds ate the strawberries under our very eyes. We were driven finally to admitting that parsley and chives scarcely constituted a fair return on the effort and so we abandoned the old, old dream. Fortunately for us, the esthetic appeal of flowers seemed lost on wild creatures—they snubbed our beautiful blossoms. Thus when our tuberous-rooted begonias began to take blue ribbons, we felt we had wiped out the disappointment about the vegetables—more or less, that is.

As mentioned earlier, my days were entirely my own and so, from the beginning of my New York life, I decided to make this time count for something. Although I like women and greatly enjoy occasional sorties with them, I was unwilling to fill my whole time with luncheons, matinees, and shopping forays. In the gargantuan anthill to which I had come to live and in which

4

I was a very small ant, I still wanted to be myself—a very individual ant, if you please. I was certain that I must draw my own pattern of activity—certain that I could not adapt any ready-made pattern. I was too young at that time to realize that the pattern I then began to draw for myself was merely a retracing of a pattern that had evolved from my childhood experiences—my likes and dislikes, my reactions, my habits. It was the old pattern laid on the new material of New York. In other words, I was reaching out for what I had been taught to value highly in my formative years.

It had been my good fortune to grow up in a home that was considerably above the average in most ways, and to receive a most thoroughgoing education along "classic" lines. My struggles with logarithmic tables, with irregular verbs, with those well-nigh unpronounceable names out of antiquity, may not have produced any immediate or practical result, but without question they gave me the lifelong benefit of a certain suppleness of mind, a kind of mental agility. The powerful force of music, which continues to be an integral part of my activities today, moved into my life when I began the study of the piano at a very early age.

Our home, I suppose, may have been regarded as more than a little worldly. To be sure, my two brothers and I knelt to say our bedside prayers, we went dutifully to the Sunday School where instruction was well-meant but brief, and our parents taught us the virtues of honesty, unselfishness, and forgiveness. We had, too, the precept left by our Grandfather Bell—"Do right and fear not." He is still saying it from the north side of his great granite monument.

My father's idea of the Good Book was a large volume of *The Complete Works of William Shakespeare*. He declared that between the covers of that volume there was as much of God as he could comprehend. From this book he would read to me, literally, by the hour, so that my young ears became attuned to the cadences of The Bard rather than to the measures of the King James Version. My rules for living came from old Polonius rather than from Sinai. It might be argued that we thus grew up under a code of ethics rather than a religious system. Perhaps. I am inclined to leave the discussion of tenets, and arguments relating to the ramifications of theological dogma to my ecclesiastical superiors. (The polysyllables are intentional, reflecting my confusion in such areas.) All I can say is home was sweet and we were a close-knit family.

As I stretched my way into my teens I experienced the usual adolescent curiosity about religion. With me this was a very private search. Gradually I became aware of a great gratitude to One who had created all the beauty and goodness to which my senses and my spirit responded. Out of this gratitude came a faith. It was a young faith, uncertain, weak, but by degrees it strengthed and became firm and solid. This was not at all like what happened on the road to Damascus. Rather, it was something that moved quietly into my life—pervasive, at once strong and gentle, for all the world like the *Char Freitag Spiel*—"Good Friday Spell"—in *Parsifal*. It was a very personal thing. I began to live by it—I still do. It is a faith of the utmost simplicity, nothing palatial, elaborate, or richly ornamented. In spite of my fondness for the Baroque in art, architecture, and music, there is nothing baroque about the structure of my faith—it is as simple as a wigwam.

Along with these various influences there was another factor in my young years which has been far-reaching and long-lasting. It is what I learned from my father, a dynamic personality. He began to teach me when I was still little more than a baby to be aware, to perceive, to feel. He encouraged me in every possible way really to see things, not merely to look at them. One of my earliest memories is involved with an instance of this.

We were walking together—my father and I—in a small wooded area near our home. I was about three years old at the time. It was a fine summer morning, filled with the music of singing birds and with shafts of bright sunlight striking down through the tall trees. Suddenly I spied something bright in the grass at our feet. In my top-heavy way I stooped and made a quick grab for it and lost my balance. As my father drew me to my feet again I clutched the desirable thing in my small fist, pulling it possessively to me.

"Flower—flower—flower" I chanted in a kind of happy sing-song. This was a long time before Gertrude Stein disclosed to the world that "A Rose is a Rose is a Rose," but I am quite certain that the same excitement of discovery prompted both outbursts.

"A flower it certainly is," said my father. "But what kind of flower?" he asked quietly.

Even now I can recall my puzzlement. This tiny yellow thing was like nothing in my mother's beautifully tended garden. But I knew all too well that when my father asked a question, he expected an answer. I scrimmaged about in my meager vocabulary and finally came up triumphantly, albeit a bit tepidly, with "Pretty flower."

My father stooped to my level and said, "Yes, it is indeed a pretty flower and you yourself found it. Now let's see how much more than pretty it is. Do you know the color?" I did.

"Very well—now we know that it is a yellow flower." Even I sensed that it was growing in significance of some kind. Then my father pointed out how symmetrical the petals were, how they curved gently away from the center.

"And have you noticed this funny little dot in the very middle? And look at this part underneath the petals. It is like a tiny green hand holding them as if they were a bouquet."

My excitement grew—how could I have known that so minute a spot of color could contain all this. I stared at it in wonder, in awe. My father, in sympathetic understanding, waited patiently for me to feast my eyes on this treasure. I recollect looking steadily at it, making, as it were, an exposure on the photographic plate of my mind, then bursting into such laughter as only a small child can indulge in—the laughter of pure delight.

"From now on we are going to find lots of things we can enjoy together," my father promised and with those words I moved into an enchanted world—the world of my father's companionship. From that time to his death—sudden, tragic, when I had just turned fifteen—he taught me the *joy* of vision. Wherever we went, he pointed out to me the singular, the exceptional. He taught me to note what lay all about me, to discern small and distinctive differences, to be conscious of the far-distant as well as the close-at-hand. I must have been an apt pupil for my playmates soon began to call me Little-Eagle-Eye and I strove mightily to deserve the nickname.

My father taught me to observe color gradations as well as those of light, variations in texture, in form. He showed me how interesting the differences in people can be—their eccentricities of manner, of gesture, of dress or carriage. He taught me to note the symmetry in some things, the lack of it in others. In short, he went beyond the idea of sight as a mere convenience and trained me in the Art-of-Seeing. In all our excursions together, this doubled our pleasure and later, when I no longer had him, this Art-of-Seeing was an incomparable traveling companion.

With such a background, it was inevitable that, when Clyde

and I went to live permanently in New York, I should seek very specific things there. I found them, and in abundance. New York can never be a lonely place or a boring one to the person who is alive to what lies about him. It offers a feast, not only for all the physical senses, but for the mind and spirit as well.

It is a wonderful thing to love the place where one lives—the place one calls home—and I came to love this many-faceted city where I was to spend the largest segment of my life. From the very beginning I was captivated by the city itself—not only by the great metropolis of today but also its historic predecessors—British New York and the Dutch New Amsterdam. Through my reading and the several remaining landmarks, these older cities came alive for me. Friends used to twit me by saying that I knew every cobblestone from the Battery to Yonkers but they were only half right for the city's environs, too, were becoming familiar to me—from the Narrows to Hawthorne Circle and beyond, from Montauk to eastern Pennsylvania where I went regularly to the great Bach and Moravian festivals.

It is always fun to share one's discoveries and knowledge with others, so I was delighted to compile a small guide book which the hotel company printed and distributed to its hundreds of guests. I filled the booklet with accurate information about the less familiar but interesting places in the city as well as those that are well known. The many expressions of appreciation which I received for this little guide made me feel useful, especially during the great World's Fair and during the War years when the city was crowded with strangers eager to "see everything."

It was fun, too, to share my musical knowledge through the Music Appreciation programs which I gave over the radio. These required considerable time for preparation but I still found time

9

to go to a cooking school to learn how to produce better meals in the country where we had little or no help.

Also during these years, I supervised the decorating of many of the hotel suites. This entailed a really professional study, for hotel decorating—unlike home decor which is highly personal— must be impersonal so as to please many types of guests. I selected furniture, carpeting, drapery materials and this gave me entree to the great wholesale houses in all these lines where I found their rich and wide variety very stimulating, very exciting.

In fact, excitement is an inherent part of New York—the city is invested with it. It is more than the excitement of the lights on Broadway, or the crowds during a ticker tape parade or gathered in Times Square on New Year's Eve. The New York excitement is of great variety and surprise. It seems to penetrate, pervade everything, touching in some way even the most prosaic, plodding lives. I was always keenly aware of this quality of excitement—all the more exciting because of its varying forms.

I could respond, for instance, to the excitement generated by the color, movement, and tension at the Belmont race track where I was often the guest of box-holding friends. It was a different kind of excitement—a hushed, awed kind—that gripped me at the Morgan Library as I looked upon the incredibly beautiful intricacies, the glowing colors, of the illuminated manuscripts, of the jewelled missals.

The great art galleries held enormous excitement for me—not only the public museums like the Metropolitan, the Modern, the Frick (the Guggenheim had not yet reared itself on Fifth Avenue)—but the commercial galleries as well. I seldom missed a new showing although my loyalty to old favorites in the permanent collections never wavered. To stand before these canvasses is to gain a fresh concept of the meaning of the word, "communication."

Pleasurable experiences came in rapid succession throughout the year—the great National Horse Show, the annual Flower Show, the Antiques Fair and many another. There was, as well, my year-round wonder at the fabulous merchandise offered in the New York shops. Perhaps my greatest joy, however, was the simple one of watching the seasons move across my two homes.

Autumn-in-New-York, for instance, is more than a pretty song. It is something you can see with your eyes. During this season a kind of coppery haze hangs over the city—a haze that now and then changes to a golden transparency that filters down among the great buildings and spills into the streets below. This is not the kind of light that bathes Paris but it is none the less beautiful. People walking through it step with a new buoyancy, a new elasticity, in anticipation. This is the season of opulence and the city tempo is stepped up. But in the country the tempo at this time would be slowing down—the land beginning its winter's rest. There we would sit in the mellow sunshine, hearing the drone of the machine filling the silos, pick out the far blue line of the Berkshire foothills, thrill to the vibrant color of the foliage. I think I always resented that the leaves of the poison ivy were the clearest, purest color of them all.

In early autumn the full moon would rise above the low Connecticut hills, floating like a huge gold balloon on a string and the whole landscape would seem to be "fixed" with a pale amber lacquer. But the full moon of late autumn rose like a thin silver disc and the night air was sharp. Next morning we would rise to look out upon the fields with a fence-to-fence carpeting of white frost. The cold light reflected from this whiteness shone on the

11

ceilings and walls of the house and gave a new dimension to everything—the colors, the shadows, even the shape of furniture. It was then time to close the house for the winter.

Winter in New York is a kaleidoscope of activity—multicolored, variformed—shaped, spaced, and keyed to the individual. An occasional blizzard may interrupt the routine of business and pleasure but it presents drama to the beholder. The cold fury of a blizzard striking New York is a spectacle one never forgets. To watch the eddying, whirling drifts of snow which the turbulent wind sends spinning and twisting among the skyscrapers is to experience a similar vertigo of one's own. The crisscross pattern made by the horizontal thrust of blast-driven sheets of snow against the perpendicular thrust of the tall buildings is a sight to make one gasp.

For most of us the peak of winter comes with the Christmas season. New York probably has the most glittering, blazing Christmas on earth but, as Christina Rossetti reminded us, "Christmas hath a lovelier beauty than the world can show." Every year I looked for this "lovelier beauty" and every year I saw it. Somewhere, apart from the tinsel, apart from the fake jewels, the fake angels, the stylized carols, I saw this Christmas look. Somewhere, in the frantically hurrying crowds along the street, or pressing about a counter, or nervously ticking off the names on a long list, I would come upon one face, so brushed with gentleness, with unselfish pleasure, with the great measure of Christmas love, that I would stop and feast my eyes upon it.

I shall always remember—and with gratitude—this look of gentleness on the face of a little old man standing before the display windows of a smart Fifth Avenue perfume shop—windows filled with sparkling "gift suggestions." He was motionless except for his eyes which moved slowly over these baubles. What was he thinking about, that old man—I wondered then and I still wonder. What was it that could put such a beautiful aura of gentleness about him—about his whole demeanor but especially about his eyes. In the eyes of that old man, a stranger, I saw the veritable Christmas.

Pleasant as it may be, winter usually outstays its welcome and when it finally takes its belated departure, spring comes in with a Nijinsky-like bound.

There is now a different whiff to the breeze as it comes up the river with the tide and the great gilt rooster atop the Heckscher building—a Manhattan Coq d'Or—which we could see from our windows, swings about with a fresh and vernal authority. Suddenly, in the streets below, the flower carts begin to appear. For, with the coming of spring, New York, along with the rest of the world, goes flower-mad. I was always interested to note the beauty-hungry look on the faces of those buying flowers—whether it was a few blooms from a vendor, a bouquet of them from a stand, or ordering armfuls of them at an exclusive Avenue florist's.

Perhaps it was because I lived in that neighborhood that I thought, from the beginning of my New York life, that the displays across from The Plaza and the Pulitzer fountain were the most colorful, the gayest of all. I often wished that Peter Brueghel might have painted the scene—he would have caught it all—the strong sunlight and the deep shadows, the spectrum of the flowers displayed on the carts, the gaiety of the passers-by. He would have captured, too, the spirit of the spring moment, the joviality of the vendors, the satisfied look of a customer hurrying away with a bit of spring bobbing in her hand. It is even possible that he would have included one of the coachmen from the old carriage line nearby as this dapper jehu tucks a blossom

13

into his coat lapel or fastens a sprig beneath the brow band of his horse's harness. I would have coveted such a canvas.

In the country, spring approached more gingerly but each weekend showed some advance. I loved the look of the countryside at every stage. I even found delight in having to sweep the house clean of acorns and nut shells which the furred, illegal occupants of the winter had left in lieu of rent. We were never able to seal the house against these "break-and-enter" rascals, the chipmunks, but they were so ingenious, so cunning, in their way of secreting their cache that we forgave them their crime, if indeed seeking shelter be counted crime.

The rataplan of the swollen brook was the overture to the pageant of spring and summer in the country. Every hour seemed to produce a new shade of green in trees and meadows—a new and lively growth. There was the usual succession of flowering shrubs and plants, the song and flashing color of the birds as they put together their versions of the split-level or cantilevered house. There was the nervous darting about of pheasants, those brilliant creatures, so lovely to look at, so painful to listen to. At night we would often see the fool's-fire flickering above the "damp place" near the willows and then one night we would catch sight of a shad-blow, in full bloom, standing motionless in the moonlight, and we would know we had looked upon the ultimate in mystic beauty.

When June came, the pink rambler rose that ran the length of the fence along the lane, would burst suddenly into its own kind of splendor. This must have been my favorite for, today, whenever the word "rose" is spoken I think pink. In the same relating way, it is a green sound that I hear when the wind rushes through the trees. Thus it is that I try to revive color in my mind, and relive it.

14

With June, too, came the lush blue-green grass in the pastures and, like sharp cutouts imposed on this vibrant green, were the black-and-white Holstein cows and their leggy calves, a plump picnic basket covered with a red-checked cloth, the great red barn near the stone wall. In Dutchess County, Mother Nature was imitating Grandma Moses.

Soon the dancers would be back at Jacob's Pillow, the music would return to Tanglewood—the country summer would be complete.

Little-Eagle-Eye had been a big girl for a long time now but at heart she was, as always, an ardent optic shutterbug, recording her "finds" on the film-roll of memory, and ever grateful for her kind of comprehension. Despite my passionate love of music, my warmest response was to the pleasurable excitement of vision. Vision was my life—I exulted in it. I knew this to a large degree while I still had sight. I know it even better now.

Late in 1952 Clyde and I found that a long-cherished dream was going to come true for us—we were to spend a month or so in the Arizona desert. We motored out, skirting the snowy midlands by following a southern route along the Gulf coast, then striking out across the long stretch of Texas to the high country of New Mexico and then to Arizona. This was not our first trip over this route but the season of the year, or something, seemed to give added interest to the landscape—new color, new perspective. For me there was, from the start, something very special about the trip and my response to the panorama was more acute than ever.

For many years one of our pleasures in motoring had been to get off to an early morning start—early enough, in fact, to savor the adventure of dawn and sunrise. On our first morning in the desert we rose two hours before dawn. No one else was stirring as we came out of our motel into the crystal-clear atmosphere of the high country. Complete silence lay over everything, not even a dog barked as we drove through the small town and then, past the last clutch of houses, came to the open desert. From that moment a kind of magic seemed to envelop us. There was no moon but starlight sifted itself over the wide expanse and in that faint light we could discern the precise, almost mathematical, spacing of the mesquite, stretching away into the mysterious distance.

Our car sped along noiselessly and, little by little, we began to sense the immensity of our surroundings. Scaled against this immensity, we were but a pair of inconsequential human specks, tucked into a mechanical contraption that scooted along like a beetle—a hard-shelled beetle with a long proboscis of light. That long feeler of light tirelessly probed ahead of us, endlessly searching and exploring.

Above the limitless expanse of the desert stretched the boundless reaches of the starry sky. Indeed one seemed to repeat the measure of the other in a kind of antiphonal response. Tonight the sky was not merely sprinkled with stars—it was crowded with them. They seemed closer to earth than I had ever known them. They might at any moment, I thought, scrape the top of the car—they seemed that close to our level.

Suddenly Clyde said, "Let's have a better look at this show," and stopped the car.

We stepped onto the floor of the desert as onto some huge spangled stage. There was a frosty feel to the air as if it had lately passed over snow fields or the snowy crests of mountain ridges. One screened its freshness through the nostrils with a tingling pleasure. We walked along the road, away from the car. We knew that the desert actually teems with life but tonight there was no evidence of it. We were in sole possession of this mighty universe of earth and sky. By some special and benevolent providence, no other car passed along the road during the time we stopped there, entranced, bewitched.

The stillness was enormous, almost palpable. If it were not for this solid stillness, I told myself absurdly, we might hear those stars crackle. I marveled at the brittle brilliance of some, the soft, tender shimmering of others. Some stars blazed in solitary splendor—those are the soloists, the prima donnas, I thought. Others formed small clusters, not unlike a string ensemble, and probably playing Mozart. Beyond and above all were the great galaxies of the Milky Way which, like a Brobdingnagian orchestra, swept us along, bombarding us with such force, such beauty, such pulsating rhythms as to make Lilliputians of our Beethoven, our Brahms. It was too overwhelming for a small human—a woman human, at that—to comprehend, even to contemplate.

I turned my gaze to the lower constellations that, at this darkest hour before the dawn, glittered along the horizon. Like a full-throated choir intoning Palestrina, they sang their praise of this night as they came near the verge of slipping away. Occasionally a shooting star arrested our attention as it made a bright dash across the sky, then disappeared—not unlike, I thought, some spectacular figure of our own world as he, to quote Mr. Shakespeare, "struts and frets his hour upon the stage, and then is heard no more."

Move about as it might, my gaze always came back to rest upon one particular star—to rest in very truth, as if I had somehow come to the end of a search, a quest. For some reason this star assumed special meaning, significance, for me. I could not have told why, but I sensed communication, as one might from Bach or El Greco or Rilke. I looked steadily at it, curious about the mood it had set up in me, reaching out for something it might bring to me. To be sure, its resplendent beauty fascinated me—its blue-white fire burning with fierce intensity, raying out in every direction to give it fantastic size. Yet I knew that what held me was more than its beauty, great as that was. I knew there was a link with something and, in a kind of spellbound quietude, I continued looking at it. Then, as if from a far distance, what I had been seeking came to me. I turned to Clyde.

"That star," I said slowly, "is like the high clear note in *Amahl and the Night Visitors,* when the little boy realizes he has been healed and now can give away his crutch."

"Very nice," said Clyde, "very nice, indeed." We watched the lovely thing a few moments longer, then Clyde, using his favorite nickname for me, said briskly, "And now, Mme Synesthesia —let us be gone."

We returned to the car and drove away. Soon the desert added a becoming pink to her beige dress as dawn crept over the scene. A heavy truck roared past us and almost at once the road came alive with traffic. As the first rays of the sun touched the cactus garden about a chuckwagon, we stopped for a husky breakfast that included my favorite Western speciality, a "short stack." People hailed each other in that jaunty, refreshed way which the first cup of strong coffee invariably induces. Breakfast was especially welcome to us who had been driving for hours. How grateful and happy I am that we made the effort on that dark chilly morning to leave our comfortable, warm beds and strike out into adventure, for I have that night's experience locked away safely in my remembrance. It was a wonderful way in which to write FINIS to my life of sight, for that was the last time I saw the fine full vault of the heavens, hung with stars, draped with the velvet mystery of the unknown and the unknowable.

A few days later, in Tucson, the serious eye trouble was discovered, diagnosed as detached retina—severe—and I was rushed to the hospital. Skillful surgery (diathermy needle), expert nursing, and weeks of the rigid immobility imposed on such cases followed, but the result was failure. Months later, and back in New York, the retina of the other eye became detached and the result was the same. Exhaustive tests failed to reveal a cause for the detachments—it may have been an inherited weakness. Whatever it was, we knew a different life faced us—my sight was gone.

There were many years between the first sight experience of the small yellow flower and that final benediction of the stars. What is especially singular, I think, is that in each instance I was companioned by one whose love and concern for me had been like a solid rock in my life—it was my father who walked with me when I found the little flower—it was my husband who stood with me when I saw my last star.

SO BE IT.

CHAPTER 2

The Dark Place

BLINDNESS is more than a physical handicap. The new-blind realize this fact very early in their new state, for there is an emotional aspect to blindness that strikes with terrific force from the beginning and continues to be an intimate part of the blind person's life.

The outcry of a new-blind person is very like that of a new-born babe—it is filled with protest, outrage, and fear. I too cried out in protest against my fate. I cried out in fright—yes, in self-pity. At first I said, "I cannot believe it," and then I said, "I will not believe it," but finally, fatigued beyond measure, I said, "I suppose I must believe it." And then the hard cold fact of the situation confronted me in its grim reality. A numbing terror fastened itself upon me when I was thus brought to realize that

I was doomed to live the rest of my life in complete darkness. There was an agonizing feeling of helplessness and dismay at the thought of going through day after day without eyesight.

But how, I asked myself, can I—to whom sight was more than to many people—I, who had photographic vision—who had always responded with such enthusiasm to everything my eyes had shown me—how could I live without sight? How could I endure the agony of having this part of my life removed, severed, amputated? How could I survive such mutilation? It is impossible, I said vehemently.

I would not listen to reminders that thousands of others down the centuries had learned to live in the darkness of blindness, although some had rebelled and never learned and some had lost their reason in their rebellion. I resented being reminded—in what struck me as dour and pious tones—of some of those who had borne blindness bravely—Samson, who must suffer himself to be led about by a lad; Homer, who left us such majestic sentiments; Milton, who, in our own language, sang out from his blindness. Neither did I want to be reminded of Handel who speaks to us through his music, nor of Helen Keller whose communication with us is perhaps the most heroic of them all. I knew the stories of every one of them. But, I said, these were persons of stature—great stature—and I was a person of small stature, shy, timid, and terribly afraid of this dark. How could I aspire even to look upon the examples such persons have set, much less presume to follow them?

My life had been filled with visual enjoyment—how could I meet every day without seeing color, form, motion? How could I endure an existence without the joy of travel, of seeing new lands and people—how could I live without my lifelong habit of and devotion to reading? And what can life mean to me without the sight of the countryside, and of my towered city? What about the practical matters of dressing myself, of feeding myself? How can I get about my own house and garden, seeing none of it, never getting a lift from the dear familiar things all about me?

My hours were filled with such questionings but there was no answer to any of them—along with complete darkness, complete silence reigned. The suggestion that I would have to live on my memories enraged me. I liked my memories but I wanted new and fresh experiences, too. And I needed eyes to do what I wanted to do, to see what I wanted to see. Could this, by any kind of measure, be regarded as an unreasonable attitude?

Someone once said that blindness consists of looking out at a blank wall, all day, every day. Blindness is worse than that. A blank wall would change, if ever so slightly, in its reflection of the day's light at different hours, and even the smoothest wall—devoid of the interest of texture—would reflect the sky's colors, and moonlight and twilight and dawn. No, blindness is more negative than a blank wall—blindness has no dimension at all. It is absolute nothingness—monumental, infinite nothingness—a zero, with the rim rubbed off.

It is like the double blank in a set of dominoes, I told myself—the big, double nothing—a vacant place, without pattern, without count, black from the very center to the outermost edges.

Yes, I told myself further, blindness is a place that is formless and void—no color, no shape, no movement. Instinctively I drew away from this dense black fog that had invaded my life, that surrounded and enveloped me. But how can one shut out such darkness? Open or closed, the eyes look upon nothing but sooty blackness. I cried out against the thing that had moved in with me, uninvited, unwanted, hated, feared, and oh, so increasingly possessive. But my cry was muffled in the thick murk of the fog.

Merciful Lord, I cried in dismay, how can I live in this monotony forever? I lashed out at the darkness but it did not lash back at me. It did not need to—it just sat quietly there, like so many huge black cats encircling me.

Into this muffled, choking atmosphere, there began to seep the horrified realization that I could not so much as see my own hands and feet, nor the rise and fall of so close a thing as my own breathing. All that had been so close, so ready at hand and—alas —so matter-of-factly accepted, was now far removed, as distant as outer space, if indeed it existed at all.

This sense of removal began to mount to a feeling of exile from everything that had constituted my life as a sighted person. In my new-blindness I was dismayed, confused, terrified, for what had happened to me had banished me to an alien world— a strange, unfriendly world, a world that seemed without hope or interest, a world in which from the start I was homesick for my native land, the land of the sighted.

Where could I draw sufficient courage to endure this expatriate life, day after day, month after month, year after weary year, haunted as I was certain to be by the recollection of what my life once had been. This abrupt disappearance of everything familiar —my freedom of action, the continuity of my life's pattern and purposes—this snatching away of my accustomed surroundings and activities—might not all this cause my very thinking to be pulled askew? To atrophy perhaps?

It was with this kind of thinking that I tortured myself in that visual silence, that chill darkness. Struggle as I might, and did, I seemed unable to resist the temptation to return again and again to such thoughts as the sure knowledge of my predicament fastened itself upon me, tighter and tighter. There was no question about it—I was trapped in this thing.

I reminded myself of nothing so much as a fly caught on a sheet of old-fashioned sticky flypaper—a fly tugging and pulling, protesting his misfortune with a mighty buzzing, and struggling all the while. I, however, was worse off than a fly so stuck, for often he can free himself by giving up a wing or leg and so effecting his escape. In my misfortune I had no comparable gamble —I had no optic wing or leg that I could risk in the hope of escaping my trap. The recollection of many fly-studded sheets brought home to me the depressing fact that it is impossible to escape the inescapable.

In my extremity, a scene from Beethoven's opera *Fidelio* flashed across my mind. In the second act the stage setting is that of a dungeon in which the heroine's husband, Florestan, has been imprisoned for several years. In this scene Florestan pours out his great agony of spiirt in the aria, *Gott, welch Dunkel hier*—"God, what darkness here." No one can listen to this aria without being shaken to the core, without a deep sense of compassion for this man who has been denied light—for all persons so denied. The impact on blind listeners is even more poignant than on the sighted, for the blind comprehend the enormity of this man's suffering. They know through experience, through identification with him, the cruelty of oppressive darkness.

I once heard a distinguished music critic say: "This aria has always seemed a little false to me. Why should this man cry out in such sudden protest at the dark, as if he were just discovering that fact? After all, he has been in that dungeon for three years and it has always been dark as midnight."

The answer to this criticism is that the cry is completely valid. Every time that Florestan peers into that darkness he is struck

24

afresh by its horror, its inevitability, and the accumulated weight of three years of it. Instead of lessening, the torment deepens with time. He has not grown used to it, and he never will, because it is not in the nature of man to live on good terms with perpetual darkness. So it is, too, with the blind. We may accommodate ourselves to our state of darkness but we never feel it is our natural habitat. Even the born-blind seem always to be reaching out for something they are certain should have been theirs.

Reliving this scene with Florestan, and steeped in his mood, I, too, cried out in despair, "Oh—God, what terrible, terrible darkness this is." I wept in fear and self-pity for I was not so brave as the patriot Florestan.

The feeling of imprisonment, however, persisted, intensified. Undeniably, I told myself, this blindness is a veritable prison—not one of these sun-flooded, glass-walled prisons of today—my prison is like the cruelest, the most hideous of all prisons, the oubliette—that fiendish place without door or window into which the prisoner was flung from the top, the roof laid over and, like a lid, clamped down. And how cunningly contrived is this word "oubliette"—the French word "oublier" (to forget), plus the diminutive "ette." This "little forgettery" was where I was to spend whatever was left to me of this life.

In the still and solid darkness the "black" wrapped me close, stifling and choking me until I gasped for very breath. It was like a mummy case, I thought, swathing and enclosing me from head to foot, encasing me with a rigid finality. At first this blackness was flat against me, pressing in nauseous proximity. As time went on, the dark began to acquire a kind of depth—plumbless depth—but there was no comfort in this feeling of space for I felt smaller and more helpless as this brutal presence assumed larger proportions. Perhaps one could reach out in this roomier phase—but reach out for what? For more of the identical blackness? In this immensity without significance, there was nothing else.

Then one day a clear certainty about my situation took possession of me—the certainty that I was helpless, powerless, finished. I was pinned beneath the debris of the calamity which had fallen upon me, debris as pressing, as suffocating as any resulting from an earthquake or a hurricane. I knew there was no strength in me to lift any part of this mass. Can anyone come to my rescue, I wondered. Can anyone reach me—can anyone even know the extent of my plight? It is unlikely.

The sad and sodden part was that suddenly, and for the first time in my life, I had no desire to make any effort to help myself. Nothing was worth the doing, nothing worth a struggle in this dead-end existence. I sank back, surrendering myself to "make my bed in Hell," as the Psalmist puts it. It does not matter, I sighed, and let myself sink slowly down into the gloom—interested in nothing, expecting nothing. I wish that I could say that at this moment the strains of that beautiful British dirge, *Flowers of the Forest*, moved through my consciousness. Music, however, had drawn away from me. Here in the darkness there was not even the slow and somber throb of a muffled drum.

CHAPTER 3

I Decide to Emigrate

I DO not know how long this dark apathy, this bleak surrender, lasted. One dreary hour was like another, all of them without interest.

"*Komm, du süsse Todes-stunde,*" I murmured, in desperation, but the phrase came out flat and empty, shorn as it was of the Bach music. "Yes—Come, sweet death," I begged, adding, "only let not my last hour be scarified by cowardice." But my plea— dry and thin as a wafer—seemed to crumble in the engulfing dark.

One day, however, I sensed within myself a small unrest. It was faint, indefinite, vague, as it nudged me. Something was disturbing the dark, the silence. In a bewildered kind of way I sought to identify it. Was this sheer boredom with the constant monotony of everything—was it some belated curiosity about my predicament—was it, perhaps, some tiny seed of decency planted in me years and years before and now stirring to life? I could not say.

I was still contained within the compress of darkness—it wrapped me close and tight. But now it seemed to be wound around me, round and round, more like a cocoon, I thought, than like a mummy case. A cocoon? The word, the idea, roused me gently. Isn't a cocoon, I asked myself with unexpected and surprising interest, better than a mummy case? Nothing ever leaves a mummy case—nothing can escape from it. From a cocoon, however, something wonderful emerges—a different kind of life —a more beautiful life. Was it possible that by some chance, some unbelievable, awesome chance, I still had life at the core of my being? And if so, might I loose myself from this cocoon of my own darkness?

Full on the heels of this question—and as sly as Iago—came the inner query: Do you want to be brought back into life, to be revived, resuscitated? Immediately self-pity and inertia replied: Let me be. A wiser, calmer voice asked: Is that what you really want? Be honest. I pondered a long while, wondering, and more than a little fearful. In the end I read my own heart clearly. I knew that I did not want to quit. I did not want to quit life nor did I want to quit a struggle that had scarcely begun.

Most of all I knew I wanted to protect, to nurture the small spark that continued to stir within me—this minuscule incandescence—this atom of invincibility—that had come into my consciousness, into my keeping. A sense of quietude came over me but it was not the quietude of despair and abandonment which had so lately and so fully possessed me. Indeed, this seemed to be a quietude of waiting. And if one waits, I whispered almost stealthily to myself, is not that an admission that one believes there is something to wait for? With unaccustomed patience I waited—but now the waiting was for something other than annihilation, obliteration.

Little by little, the fog of my thinking lifted and I realized with an ever-strengthening conviction, that this small stirring in the vast gloom was my own Self—the very heart of my being that had never surrendered.

It was about this time that a further truth about my predicament revealed itself. Up to now the great darkness that imprisoned and tormented me had seemed "all of a piece" but I began to perceive that this was not true. This dark was in actuality composed of two elements—the physical blindness which, like a black monster, I would have as my companion for the rest of my life, and the emotional darkness, the gloom that had enclosed my spirit—and understandably so—ever since the physical blindness had moved into my life.

For some time I had realized that the Black Beast—the *bête noire*—would have to be figured in on every plan I made, every move I made, even my most secret wishes. I might as well become reconciled to the fact that I could not rid myself of him.

The emotional dark, however, was a thing apart from him— and I began to examine this aspect. Must this, too, be a lifelong association? Was it not possible, in some way, to take my new-found Self out of this pitch-black despondency—to flee this "oubliette" of heaviness of spirit? The more I mulled over the idea, the more convinced I became that there might be a way. There must be an exit somewhere, I argued—a little trap door, or a hidden secret passage that will lead me out of this condition. After weeks in this state I could understand how persons, confined to dungeons, became insane or overcome with such apathy that they were worse than dead. My emotional dungeon was just as real to me as stone walls and iron bars. Prisoners, I recalled, often burrow tunnels beneath thick impenetrable walls and so escape. Was this possible to me? I will try anything, everything, I vowed, for escape I must. By then I knew with solid certainty that I could never, would never, be content to settle down permanently in this desolated place of inactivity and nothingness— settle down for what unthinking persons chose to refer to as "the rest of your life." Life? That kind of life for me? It would not be life at all—it would, in fact, be worse than the stillness of death.

I now know that my desire, my impulse, at that time, was not a reaching out toward something—it was essentially a propulsion from something. I was operating on the negative side of everything. My only cry was, "Let me out." It never occurred to me that at some later time I might come to a place where I would call out, "Let me in."

My immediate concern, however, was for my newfound Self. Suppose I could not hold on to this new and fragile hope that had risen within me? Suppose I prove not strong enough to tend this tiny flame, scarcely more than a spark? How can I make even a beginning in this hideous darkness—here where I cannot see even one step ahead?

I was thinking along these lines one afternoon months later when the first answer to my questioning came—suddenly, dramatically. I had been left alone for a while and was comfortably settled in the living room. The room had not been changed in any way and should have provided me with the familiar and pleasant ambiance it had always held for me. But now it seemed empty of everything I had known—empty and strange. I had been told that there were fresh flowers in the room, but inasmuch as they

30

were without fragrance they were meaningless to me. I could not see, and so respond to, the soft colors, the mellow tones of the furniture, the easy comfortable lines of sofa and chairs. Nor could I see the sparkle of mirrors, the view from the windows. To me none of it was there—blindness had blotted it out. There is enormous and painful shock to the person catapulted from a life of sight into the vacuity of blindness and, on that afternoon, I was poignantly aware that my own living room was now as impersonal, as unrelated, as a storage warehouse.

A miserable fear began to creep around me, to sneak into my thinking. I shivered a little and the fear tightened its chilly hold on me. I knew that all too often panic lies just beyond such fear and I was determined that panic—a vicious and uncontrollable thing—should not seize upon me. What can I do to avoid this? My thoughts were chasing each other at terrific speed now—the emptiness was menacing. Before this mounting fear, this spiraling dread, turned into unholy terror I was given the good sense to know that I should talk to someone. I should hear a human voice in this room which to me was so vacant of everything, so dark, so quiet.

An idea came. The telephone, I cried in relief. Through the telephone I could bring a human voice into this place—and at once. Perhaps that is what I miss, what I need. I will call Cécile.

I groped my way across the room, fumbled for the telephone. I sat down and picked up the receiver. At that very instant my life as a blind woman began—my first real problem in blindness confronted me.

I had not the faintest idea of how to dial a phone without seeing it. I was appalled. I so desperately needed to hear Cécile's voice and now I was blocked. I ran my fingers over the dial. I knew there were numbers and letters there, but how were they arranged? Why had I never memorized this gadget? Why were we not taught useful things like this in school? I turned from the phone, ready to accept defeat. But my desire to speak with Cécile was so compulsive that I turned back. Along with my mounting urge to get in touch with my friend, there was forming within me a small rebellion, and it began to grow—a rebellion not against the blindness as much as against this uncooperative contrivance that had been so easy to use when I had sight. I knew that I was not ready to accept defeat. I knew, too, that nothing could defeat me unless I permitted it to defeat me. I quieted myself.

I seemed to recall that the operator's signal was next to the finger stop. I would try. It was no small miracle to me when, from out of nowhere, a bright young voice answered. I explained that I was new-blind and alone, and would she be so good as to tell me how the letters and numbers are arranged on the dial so that I might make a call. Oddly enough, and certainly for my future good, it did not occur to me to ask the operator to make the connection for me. If I had done that, I might have set a pattern of helplessness that would have been difficult to erase. The bright young voice carefully explained the distribution of letters and numbers and, ten minutes and four wrong numbers later, I heard Cécile's animated voice. By that time, however, I no longer actually needed her. I enjoyed speaking with her as I always do, but the sharp need for her had somehow been lost during the time I was wrestling with the little turntable. I had become so engrossed with helping myself—with taking myself out of helplessness—that the need for outside help no longer existed.

When I had put down the receiver, I felt my way back to the sofa and sat there quietly for a long while, reviewing what had just happened. A kind of happy elation spread through me—not only because of this initial small victory but because my first rebellion against helplessness had triggered an explosion—an explosion that had cracked the very walls of my emotional prison. Furthermore, I was certain that if I persisted in rebelling against helplessness, other explosions would occur, making wider cracks in these walls that had been enclosing me—enclosing me with a choking sense of deprivation, of self-pity, of uselessness, of complete divorcement from every activity of my sighted life. The experience at the telephone had shown me that I still had capacities that I could rely on—that there must be countless ways in which I could help myself.

Mysteriously I began to feel at home again in my own living room that up to now had seemed so alien. I deliberately summoned up a picture of how it must look. I even reached out and touched the flowers. True, they had no fragrance but there was about them a kind of green-growing scent. I found pleasure in trying to imagine their color. This was a novel and surprising turn for one who had until this hour felt "deader than dead." I marveled that my first attempt to do something for myself had accomplished this glowing result. It was right then and there that I made a solemn promise to myself, a firm resolve—which so far I have been able to keep—that in this new way of life I would never ask anyone to do for me anything that I could learn to do for myself. I would ask help only after I had exhausted all my own resources.

My first step had proved, in a beginning kind of way, that I was not permanently bound to a condition of dark helplessness. It followed then that what I was not bound to, I could get away from, escape from. But how was this to be effected? I was now in a real huddle with myself. Most people, I said, when they come to loathe a place, try to emigrate from it. At once I knew I had what I was looking for—it was that word "emigrate" and what it represented. I turned it over in my mind as I might turn over a bright coin in my hand, over and again. It fascinated me. The old Latin derivation was so clear—"e"(ex), away from, out of, plus "migro," to move. There it was—to move away from, to leave. What a beautifully apt word, I exclaimed—and that is precisely what I shall do—"emigrate" from this foul place, this emotional coal pit in which I have loitered overlong, in an atmosphere which is not natural for me. Again my interest, my consideration, was not that eventually I would reach some special, some particular region. It was wholly the thought of escaping this one. I saw that the Dark Place was not only an area of torment but there was also about it something of shame. I could not think of it now without a blush of chagrin that I had permitted myself to remain there as long as I had. Immediately and resolutely my back, like the backs of all true emigrants, was turned against the place I was quitting. I must make up for all that lost time, I said. I must take this newfound Self and begin my emigration, my journey.

And what about the Black Beast? I asked myself, half-mockingly. In this fine resolve, have you forgotten him?

Not at all, I answered myself. I know full well that he will go with me. I may not bring myself to Dancing-in-the-Dark with the Beast but neither will I waste time and energy fighting with him. One thing is certain—on this journey I cannot afford the excess baggage of resentment against him. It may even be possible to make an ally of him and, who knows, I may learn a great deal from him. I spoke more wisely than I knew, for I have learned a great deal from the Beast—this handicap of blindness.

At about this point in my planning a visitor was announced, a friend whom I truly love. She is a person not only of great wit and charm but of a sympathetic understanding as well. I told her of what I had been thinking and at once she said, "Now, my dear, before you go a step farther, I want you to do one thing. I want you to go quietly and alone to your own room, get down on your knees and ask God to bless this blindness."

"What?" I cried, "Bless a curse?" Of all the things that had been recommended to me, this was without question the maddest of all. I wanted to break into laughter at the idea—perhaps I did. She merely said,

"Do this to please me, if for no other reason. Any burden that is blest through sincere petition is transfigured—it never fails."

I promised that I would do as she asked although I fear I had my fingers crossed about the whole matter but, because I believed in the counsellor if not in the counsel, I later did what she had asked. I stayed upon my knees until I could make the petition in complete honesty. The moment came when the prayer left off being perfunctory and became sharply focused, clear, steady.

As I rose to my feet I felt somewhat as the old Crusaders must have felt when, after their benediction, they set off on their long journey. But how much more spectacular and colorful were those adventurers than I could be. They had bright banners, gay minstrels, richly caparisoned horses—no, I am sure theirs were "steeds"—while I was a lone woman, unaccompanied by fanfare, knowing not even one marching song. One thing we had in common, those old Crusaders and I—hate. They hated the Infidel—I hated the Dark Place.

And so I set out—cradling the small flame in my arms, dragging whatever luggage of the spirit I could manage, and burdened with the Beast. The Beast was not, like the Mariner's albatross, slung about my neck. Instead, he sat on my shoulders, his paws across my eyes, hot and pressing. He was a heavier bur-

35

den than any albatross, as I shall tell the old mariner if I ever chance upon him along the way.

I was certain there would be problems—there always are—but I was also certain that for each of these there would be a solution. More than likely there would be difficulties and disappointments. It was even possible that I would not get very far on this journey but I knew that I wanted to make a start. In fact, the journey had really begun with that telephone call.

CHAPTER 4

My Journey Begins

THUS with my face turned resolutely away from the Dark Place I began to wonder what my first step on this journey should be. Admittedly I was bewildered, but from out my consciousness there swam up to me something laid away there a long time ago. It was an Old English admonition and I welcomed it as a friend. "Do Ye Nexte Thynge," it said—in other words, the nearest thing, the thing that lies closest to hand.

Directly I knew what should be my "nexte thynge." It was to look after my own personal needs—to groom and dress myself, to reacquire ease and skill at table. To do these things for myself would not only give me a considerable measure of satisfaction, but would also release those who had been doing so much for me, albeit, let me hasten to say, with the greatest affection. Far and above these considerations—and they were not small—would be the lightened hearts of those about me to observe this first faint show of interest on my part; to observe, too, my evident desire to escape the pernicious shuttling between terror and lethargy. If only to hearten them, I would make this beginning.

I used to wonder how blind persons could find their clothes and dress themselves. Actually it can be the essence of simplicity. Each garment has its own particular "feel" and one soon learns to recognize it by touch as readily as one formerly did by sight. In fact, in one way it is easier—we blind never need to turn on a light to find what we want from the clothes closet or dresser drawer. To be sure, there is a bit of memory work connected with this but that is part of keeping ourselves fit. Memory, like other machinery, can best be kept in working order through constant use.

Simple as it has become for me now, I can never forget the devastating feeling of helplessness that engulfed me the first time, after becoming blind, that I tried to dress myself unaided. I was alone, wearing a negligee when I decided to change before my husband's return.

I groped my way to my clothes closet—felt along the row of dresses hanging there. Surely, I thought in dismay, none of these could be mine. There was nothing familiar about any of them. I was completely baffled until my fingers actually touched one garment which I recognized by its rough texture. I would start with this. I slipped into it, zipped it up, then remembered there should be a belt to match. My belts were kept in a compartmented box—could I, I wondered, find the right one? I touched every belt—they might have belonged to somebody else. I turned my attention to locating proper shoes and confusion was "twice confounded."

At this point the temptation to give up the whole idea was strong. How could I ever learn what I thought I already knew— my own wardrobe. If this blindness had moved in on me gradually, instead of striking without warning, I could have prepared myself for adjustment to a new condition. At this moment, however, the desire to look nice for my husband, the desire to try to make him forget that I was no longer the same as before, overcame the inclination to quit. I guessed at a belt and put on some shoes. I got neither the belt nor the shoes I hoped I was getting, but luck was with me, for when Clyde came in he asked,

"Oh, who helped you dress?"

"I grew up today, I'll have you know, and I dressed myself."

"Wonderful," he exclaimed, "and I like the red belt and red shoes with that dress."

I was happy that this excursion into activity had turned out well, but I knew that in the future I should have to trust to something more reliable than mere luck. I must set up a workable system that would enable me to lay hands, unerringly, speedily, on whatever I wanted from that closet. Of one thing I was sure—with each dress I would hang its own belt.

With the help of a friend I spent considerable time arranging and memorizing the clothes I had on hand. These would last me quite a while and new clothes could be a future worry. I soon learned that my best dependence lay in the texture of the material and some identifying feature—pleats in a skirt, self-covered buttons, the rustle of a taffeta skirt lining. She and I also attacked the problems of my dresser drawers, setting up a simple arrangement for lingerie, gloves, hosiery, and sweaters. The only real difficulty was the sweaters. One plastic bag is much like another to the touch—the trick was to devise a system to identify

39

the color inside each bag. Every plan seemed to result in something as intricate and complicated as the Queen's Cipher. I still have trouble with those sweaters and usually have to ask for help. Some problems, it would seem, are difficult of precise solution when one of the essential tools is missing. It took months, for example, for me to acquire efficiency in shampooing, rinsing and setting my hair—in effecting satisfactory manicures and pedicures, in applying the slight make-up I use. I have, however, grown less tense about these things and the results are better.

Along with these first exercises in dressing, I was also learning to feed myself. Because I had heard of blind persons who must be fed every mouthful and of others who were so untidy in their eating habits as to render themselves "personae non gratae" even in their own family circle, I had an understandable horror of what might lie ahead of me in that direction. So in those earliest days of my emigration from the Dark Place I began to make the first fumbling effort to eat like a human adult and not like an infant nor an animal.

It was discouraging—endlessly discouraging—not only because progress seemed slow but because—and this was the incredible, almost unendurable part of it all—what had been practically automatic in my sighted days now had to be thought out in every detail. Only two things from my sighted experience at table continued to be automatic now—keeping my elbows close to my body and keeping my mouth closed while chewing. Everything else had to relearned. I felt at times that another dimension was involved, for food does not feel the same to the tines of a fork as it looks to the eye. Formerly my eye could instantaneously inform my brain what was on the plate, but now this information must be relayed over a circuitous route, via the fork, my hand, my arm and so to my brain. With time this message service has speeded up but at first it was painfully slow. No young child was ever more severely drilled in table manners than I drilled myself in those first months of my journey—during what might be termed my second kindergarten days. This time was devoted to the simplest dining operations—I did not permit myself to think of anything but immediate necessity.

Early in my struggles at the table I adopted the method used by many blind persons of visualizing the dinner plate as a clock dial. A sighted person describes the items and their location on the plate in some such fashion as—"The roast beef is from five to seven o'clock, mashed potatoes are at two o'clock (and be careful of the gravy), the string beans at noon, beets at ten o'clock." Thus the blind diner knows not only "what's for dinner," but also how to plan his attack, for strategy is involved in the eating of every meal.

From the start liquids presented difficulties, to say nothing of hazards. For instance it was impossible for me to establish which way a cup or tumbler was tilted—and they always seemed to be tilting. I early discovered that by merely touching the glass or cup with the forefinger of my left hand, I could steady it to the point of getting at least a sip. This solution to the problem made me feel less gauche than grasping with both hands.

In the beginning I permitted someone else to cut meat for me but this soon grew intolerable for I spent too much time and nervous energy chasing those bits of meat around my plate. I gradually grew more skillful in cutting my own so that now I am comfortable knowing that the only bit of unattached meat is safely impaled on my fork.

Since our meals were served privately in our suite, I could take time in gaining mastery and confidence. I often recalled the remark attributed to a toothless old woman who declared she

41

liked okra because it was so easy to eat. I found myself tempted to order such easy-to-eat foods. I shall never forget what good friends pureed vegetables and plain ice creams were in those days.

There was, however, much enforced idleness throughout the day—a new and discomfiting experience for one who had heretofore been so active. Friends were wonderfully kind. They came frequently and never stayed too long. They brought books and magazines to read to me—one blessed friend always offered to read something of my own choosing. Others brought me small gifts, tidbits, flowers. That fragrance was now my chief interest in flowers was taken into consideration in their choice. I was deeply touched by, and most appreciative of all these reachings-out to help me.

The gift that gave me the most long-lasting delight—a parakeet—was brought by two dear friends of imaginative thoughtfulness. A bird was an innovation with us and at first I was more than a bit doubtful about how it would work out, but within twenty-four hours after his arrival, this little fellow had made a place for himself in our home and hearts. His beauty was described to me—a chartreuse body, a bright blue tail—but for me his beauty lay in his aptitudes, his affection.

Among my visitors were several children and when they saw the new bird they were curious to know what kind he was. When seeking to amuse them, we said he was a Budgerigar—they stumbled, having as much difficulty in pronouncing such a formidable word as I have in spelling it. At once they shortened it to Budgy. This was acceptable to us but when I attempted to teach the cocky little creature that his name was Budgy he balked and pronounced the word to suit himself, BUTCH. Moreover he continued to stand his ground with masculine, almost ferocious, tenacity. It was like trying to persuade a left-handed

42

person to become right-handed. I finally gave up, fearing some kind of bird-brained frustration. The result was that he remained BUTCH for all of his seven years. How he and I learned together is touched on in a later chapter of this book.

Clyde and I felt that as soon as possible I should try to go out among people again but when we ventured to do so, the theater proved a blank for me and the Ballet was pure torture. In the streets I was disturbed by the jostling of the crowds, the precarious footing everywhere, the roar and scream of traffic. Heretofore none of these things had troubled me. Now the mounted police who had always seemed such glamorous symbols of safety caused me great uneasiness, the authoritative clop-clop of their horses' hooves were menacingly close. When we went to the country, things were even more painful. So much of the pleasure there had been visual and its obliteration for me became almost unbearable, try as I might to enlarge upon the pleasure derived through the other senses. Clyde sought to divert me by taking me for drives along my favorite country roads but, aside from a general feeling of forward motion, I was just swaying about in a black tunnel—but with this difference, in this tunnel there was no heartening pinpoint of light at the far end, a pinpoint that you knew would widen and brighten until finally you would emerge into full daylight. The only light in this darkness was my husband's glowing concern for me—of this I was ever conscious. The tunnel feeling persists when I drive about the country today, but now I have learned to note the seasonal smells, the seasonal sounds.

I know now that in those early days I was too newly blind, too weakly convalescent in my new state, to have essayed so early a return to the old interests and routines. I should have known that I could not return entirely to that life—this was something I had to learn. Too, both Clyde and I began to see how our life had been disrupted, how completely everything was turned upside down, inside out. The old pattern had been destroyed for both of us. When we surveyed the future, it looked bleak, even blank.

Clyde had been considering an early retirement and, after much earnest thought, we came to the decision that we might as well make the break now. We then came to the further decision—even to us a startling one—to leave New York. Taking into account that our income would be substantially reduced after retirement, we felt it would be wise to go to live in some less expensive area, a quieter place, perhaps a milder climate. We explored the merits of several parts of the country but in the end we decided upon the small southern town where we now live. We had no acquaintance here, no letters of introduction, but neither did we have any prejudices. The deciding factor was that a large university is located here and we felt that this feature would make life fuller, more pleasant for us. We still think that, for our own particular needs and interests, we chose well.

The decision itself was, as is usually the case, the most difficult part but carrying out the details brought on by the decision was laborious and often tedious. We sold the country property and placed its furnishings and those of the city apartment in storage until such time as we should send for them. Then, after some difficult leave-taking, we drove away in our new small car. That car was a kind of symbol—life was going to be different for us and we knew it, but we had set a course and we meant to keep to it. Curiously enough, the date of our departure coincided with the date on which we had left for the desert two years before.

We took a small apartment while we searched for a house. Clyde wished me to accompany him in this search, not only because I could raise, and at once, the questions all women tend to ask about residential properties, but also because he felt that staying alone for hours would be dull for me. The local radio programs were unfamiliar and Butch was proving poor company these days for, upset by the trip and the strange surroundings, he apparently had taken the vow of silence.

The house-hunting covered an anxious span of weeks. With the help of a woman real estate broker—a soft-spoken, understanding person whom I grew to love—we looked at every available property. To clump about these strange premises, straining to visualize and memorize what each offered, trying to find an adequate, sound structure in a good neighborhood, in the price bracket we had set, would send me back to the apartment fatigued, confused, almost in despair. Each evening we would review what we had inspected to date and often this was a tedious process. I could recall room arrangements fairly well but when Clyde would refer to "the house set in a grove of pines," or "the one with bright pink shutters," or "the one on the corner lot with a viburnum hedge," I could not follow him. I identified the houses mostly by their individual smells, always definite and sometimes very strong. Naturally Clyde could not follow me in this kind of identification. This was the first time that I realized that my awareness through the sense of smell had been stepped up. At times this is a dubious asset.

The masonry house we finally bought lured us with its setting —tall pines, live oaks—one of them over ten feet in circumference—a loquat tree that was in fragrant bloom at the time, and the azaleas and gardenias common in this area.

Shopping facilities were at a considerable distance but the university campus only a block or so from us, in fact close enough for us to hear the play of the carillon, the marching band at the ROTC parades, the roar of cheering from the big stadium. We have found this closeness to "Gown" very pleasant, very stimulating.

Our household goods finally arrived and the van men, expert and obliging, distributed things throughout the house. There was left, however, the usual mountain of boxes, barrels, and packing cases to be gone into later. After the men had left I detected a note of desolation in Clyde's voice—I knew he was experiencing a real letdown.

"How," he groaned, "are we ever going to dig out of this confusion, this jungle?" Like most men, his inclination was to run from such clutter and, like most women, I wanted to start in and straighten everything—at that very moment, in fact.

"Just give me a few days and this place will be home," I promised him.

"But, dear," he countered, "you forget things are different with you now. With the best will in the world you cannot be the autogyro you once were."

There it was—laid right on the line for me—and I felt the burden of the Beast with his paws on my eyes. "You are right, of course," I told him, "but that is only on the outside. Inside I am the same." I was talking brave—I knew that only too well—but I also knew that I was going to keep this newfound self safe, protected. I must stop my ears against negative suggestion—must reach out for a "nexte thynge." We sat for quite a while without talking—the long-married feel no necessity to break such silences with mere talk. After some time Clyde said,

"I was just recalling what Helen said when she came to say good-bye. Remember?"

I remembered. Helen had said, "I marvel at what you two are

46

doing—taking yourselves from the life you have had for so long, from friendships of many years' standing, from activities that still might mean so much to you—to go to a strange place and live among complete strangers, and with this newly inflicted handicap. Oh, what courage you have."

With the weight of the whole undertaking suddenly bearing down upon him Clyde said, "I wonder—is it courage or just plain foolhardiness?"

"That way lies danger," I quoted to myself and hastened to reassure my husband. "We must not let doubt creep in at this point. Our decision to come here was not made hastily, and I still think it was a wise decision." When he made no reply I went on, "I must tell you something else. I have not spoken of this before because I did not want it to influence you in the decision to leave New York, but I have been troubled, during these months of blindness, by the way our friends have tended to over-protect me in various ways, from various things. They were really suffocating me with kindness and attention—they pitied me so, even cried over me. I appreciated their concern but it began to oppress and weaken me. Here, where we know no one, I start fresh—for me this is the beginning of a new life. Any acquaintances we make here will know me only as a blind woman —I must stand or fall on what I can do for myself here and now, not on what I was in the past. If I am to grow in this new condition, I am going to have to learn new ways. I believe this very fact is going to be galvanizing for both of us. Actually, I am beginning to be excited over what lies ahead."

"Maybe so—maybe so." Clyde was only half-convinced. "But this place, my dear, is utter confusion. If you could see it, you would feel gloomy, too. And tell me, whatever can be in all those boxes? There are thirty-seven of them, by actual count, and the labels have only a few hieroglyphics scratched on them." He began to pace the length of the room. "Can't we get somebody to unpack all this right away? I can't stand the sight of it, sprawled around like this."

"Tomorrow morning," I promised him, "I will get help through an agency. Not knowing when the van would arrive, I could not definitely engage anyone beforehand. Once we start unpacking the stack will melt away quickly. Don't fret yourself —everything will smooth out."

The words were scarcely off my tongue before there was a rap at the rear porch door and when Clyde went to answer it, the deep voice of a Negro man rumbled out.

"I see the movers leaving, sir. Would the lady like a good maid to help her get straightened out? My wife is a real good maid and she has some extra time."

I had never before employed anyone without asking for references, but something in the boom of that "Big Ben" voice made me trust him.

"Tell her to come tomorrow morning," I said.

The big voice turned its attention to my husband. "I know a good yard man, sir. He'll fix your place fine for you." Clyde told him to send the yard man the next day.

"I know a good concrete man too, sir—if you're thinking about fixing that driveway." The concrete man was bidden to come.

He left and we fell to laughing. "I wonder what the name of his agency is," chuckled Clyde, "and what other services he can command."

Our laughing had broken the tension—we relaxed. "Maybe," I said hopefully, "there are only thirty-six boxes after all. Why don't you count them again?"

Clyde did not answer, for the simple reason that he was no longer in the room. I had not yet learned to listen for footsteps to tell me when persons come and go. I heard him whacking away at some kind of crate in the garage. Shortly afterward he came back to announce that, having noticed so many birds about the place, he thought they might enjoy the birdbath, so he had set it out on the lawn. It is quite a large one but sits low to the ground. He had filled it with water and now he reported,

"It already has customers—I see two redbirds—now there are four sparrows—and oh, here comes one of those streamlined mocking birds. These fellows are really thirsty, and bathing like crazy."

A fine glow spread through me. Doubt and hesitation, even a kind of homesickness had been routed.

We went back to the apartment for the night but returned early the next morning. We had been there only a few moments when there was a soft rap at the door and a gentle voice said, "I'm Mazie. I've come to help you." As simply as that Mazie came into our life and she has been part of it ever since. Quiet, gentle, punctual and never-failing, I still wonder how we merit such devotion. Perhaps we don't.

Although she could give us only half of each day, Mazie and I brought considerable order out of the chaos within a week. I think I could not have stood up under a full day's work for, although Mazie could do many things on her own, there was much that I alone must do in order to know later on where everything had been stored. For instance, she could clean shelves and line them with paper but I myself had to place everything on those shelves—bed linen and towels and blankets in the linen closet, china and crystal in the kitchen cupboards, cooking utensils in the pantry. Every day we emptied boxes and barrels and yet Clyde claimed the house was overrun with them—it reminded him of the overflow of water in *The Sorcerer's Apprentice.*

By the second week our efforts began to show encouraging results. Mazie had washed all the windows, waxed the furniture, polished silver and brass and laid the rugs. Best of all she had, in her quiet way, made friends with Butch—had persuaded him to talk again. In fact, he was now chattering constantly as he surveyed all the activity about him with evident approval.

Mine was the challenging job of placing the furniture. This took an enormous amount of visualizing—to balance the large pieces against the smaller, to bring accent colors into proper and pleasing relation with the main colors, to establish the best grouping for comfort and convenience as well as appearance. To accomplish all this with only imagination, the fingertips, and a yardstick with which I could of course merely approximate measurements, required all the concentration and persistence I was capable of.

Little by little confidence and skill were developing within me although there were many times when I felt the pull, like that of a strong magnet, back toward the Dark Place. I came to recognize this for what it was—the pull of discouragement, an unwanted thing. I learned, too, that the best way to break its force was to begin another "nexte thynge" at once.

At this point in our settling in, a rather startling "nexte thynge" presented itself. Our house was now complete except for one feature—draperies. The necessary yardage for these—a beautiful *Toile de Jouy*—had been sent down by my favorite importer and a local woman had been engaged to make the draperies. Now we had word that she had been called out of town and would likely be away for many weeks. I was unable to locate anyone else who could do the work.

I admit it was downright silly of me to be so concerned about uncurtained windows but I believe most women can understand my perturbation. Those draperies were all that stood between me and the completion of this present project. I became restless about the matter and every time I thought about those yards of beautiful toile lying on the closet shelf I grew even more restless. So close was I to finishing what I had begun, and now I was blocked. Not only was I irked by the bareness of my windows but as well by the subtle inference that this bareness pointed up my dependence, my helplessness. Finally, vexed and—yes—angry at this delay, I decided to do them myself. I am sure that anger is not a good approach, like a gangplank, to accomplishment and I do not recommend it. I am merely reporting that in this instance it worked.

I had been expert at handsewing since I was a little girl and I was so sure of my ability to make those draperies that I could see no objection to my trying. Clyde was appalled at the idea. I had to use all the persuasion I was capable of to get him to agree to my making the attempt. With that hurdle negotiated, I measured off the necessary lengths with the faithful yardstick, drew threads to even the cloth, and Mazie cut along the drawn thread. She also cut off the selvage. With a notched piece of cardboard I measured hems and set to work. It took time, endless patience—thread can become as knotty as any world problem— but after days of dogged determination the curtains were finished, ready for pressing and hanging. The fact that lined draperies are not desirable in this climate simplified the task immeasurably. When the fixture man had adjusted them on traverse rods and

I heard their soft swish as they swung into place, I could have shouted for joy. I ran my fingers along the smooth flat hems. This, I said to myself, is true blind-stitching.

During the next few hours I experienced a very happy mutation. Up to this time I had had the persistent feeling of being an exile in this strange house which I had never seen, would never see—an exile yearning for home. I was perplexed that this feeling should continue after our various possessions were disposed throughout the rooms. Indeed, even these very objects seemed strange and alien—they seemed to retain little connection with our previous life. Why, I asked myself, do I not feel at home here? With the hanging of the curtains, however, which in a way symbolized the end of my responsibility in establishing this new home, this feeling began to dissipate itself.

As I made my way from room to room, touching this object and that, I sensed that I was regaining my former association with them. Even the lamps, with their familiar click or pull and whose light I could not see, gave out a warmth that I could feel. Suddenly I realized that the pressure of responsibility had kept me from the very thing I wanted—the feeling of belonging here. I sank down into my favorite little French chair and ran my fingers along the smooth worn carving. The chair's well-loved contour seemed to invite me, welcome me. I relaxed—at last I had "come home." The little flame of my Self burned clear and steady. The Beast's paws seemed to press less heavily on my eyes. I felt that I had proved, if only to a small degree, that I was not useless.

This was further brought home to me that evening as we sat listening to one of our favorite Bartok recordings. When the music was finished, Clyde remarked,

"I'm beginning to like this place—it really feels like home now. You've done a good job, darling."

The Dark Place of inactivity and self-pity, of gloom and inertia, was for the moment far off—a bad dream, perhaps—but I had sense enough to know that it still might insinuate itself into my life and that I must be ever on the alert, ever vigilant.

CHAPTER 5

My Journey Continues

MAZIE had told us that, after she had settled us in, she could come to us only part time each week. We had agreed to this arrangement feeling we could "do" for ourselves in between times. Obviously, our first consideration was the question of meals. My cooking-school knowledge and somewhat limited experience were swept aside at once by my husband who had a great fear of my being anywhere near a stove. To my astonishment he announced he was going to do the simple cooking we would need. That word "simple" misled me, for it soon developed that for years he had wanted to have a fling at kitchen cooking—he had never had any interest in being a backyard griller.

I therefore turned over to him my collection of recipes and he embarked, with no little bravura and no timidity whatever, on the *Haute Cuisine*. He was pleased to have the recipes but he declared that any recipe was only a guide—that if one used a pinch of this and a handful of that, plus imagination, singular results could be achieved. True, his initial concoctions were singular, but we ate them. He persisted in his efforts and in his conviction that he had a real flair for putting together a good meal. Now, after several years, his success is little short of spectacular. To me the most astounding aspect of this venture has been the patience with which he has addressed himself to something I would have guessed was completely foreign to his nature. This might go a long way in proving how little a wife really knows about her husband, for I never suspected this deep-seated desire to emulate the great Escoffier.

He contended from the beginning that one of the secrets of topflight cookery lies in having all ingredients fresh. We must market every day, he announced. We therefore went regularly to buy each day's provisions. I could not have agreed more with him about the desirability—the necessity—of fresh ingredients but I was skeptical about such frequent marketings. This is all right in France where it is the custom and where one comes almost to knowing the name of the hen that lays the few eggs you buy each day. Our American supermarkets are more, shall we say, impersonal and our home refrigerators, even the smallest, will care for several days' provisions. The time-consuming aspect of this daily marketing finally tipped the scales in favor of twice-a-week forays. I enjoy these trips. Clyde calls off the contents of the bins,—fruits, vegetables, the displays of meats, cheeses and so on. Knowing thus what is offered, I can be more helpful in planning the menus.

In negotiating the comparatively narrow aisles usual in supermarkets, it is well-nigh impossible for us to walk side by side. To walk tandem, with me trailing my *liege,* would be to defeat my purpose in coming along, which is to consult and help decide what our purchases shall be. We have, therefore, hit upon a kind of compromise between these two positions and I now walk a bit to the "southeast" of him, as it were. I have the absurd habit of grasping one of the belt loops on his slacks as we move along. This more or less enables me to synchronize my pace with his.

One day, when we had an unusually long list of items, we thought to save time by my remaining with the cart, near the vegetable counter while Clyde darted about to other areas for items where no decision was involved. We often do this. After a short time I felt the cart being moved along slowly and a form pressed close to me reaching among the vegetables. Believing it was my husband I reached for the belt loop and slipped my finger through it. In doing so I became sharply conscious that he was getting fat to the point of revulsion. Giving the loop a tug for emphasis I said,

"Darling, you have simply GOT to go on a diet. You are disgustingly fat."

A high Gilbert-and-Sullivan tenor—not my husband's baritone—answered me.

"I know it, honey, but I just love to eat."

Horrified, I snatched my finger from this stranger. Just then Clyde returned and I gasped,

"Oh, I've done the most awful thing."

"Not at all—not at all," Gilbert-and-Sullivan declared. "The lady has just given me some good advice, but I probably won't take it."

All of us broke into laughter and the man, Clyde reported, waddled off in the direction of the Danish pastry. Ah, well.

Clyde's initiate cooking days are far behind now and he revels

56

in his new skill. I like what he cooks and I like also his economy in the use of cooking utensils, for you see I became the dishwasher in this household. I still am. Perhaps I am a bit slow about this but my breakage record is commendably low. I find I must work alone at this for I have a routine of placing dishes in the sink and on the cupboard shelves. I can do all this skillfully unless someone attempts to "help" me. Then I am utterly routed.

The job of bedmaking naturally fell to me and at first it never occurred to me that this might involve any real difficulty. In fact I approached my first "go" at this with considerable confidence. I stripped the beds, brought fresh sheeets and pillowcases from the linen closet. Shaking a sheet free of its folds, I spread it across the bed but I was unable to get it smooth. There were wrinkles everywhere. What could be causing this, I wondered. I thought I knew how to make a bed but in this new darkness it appeared I did not know the first thing about it. I ran my fingers here and there and twitched at the corners—things got worse. Then I stood beside that bed as a doctor might stand beside a patient, diagnosing the trouble. The answer came—the trick was to center the sheet. And why had I not thought of this before? Because, I suppose, I was still operating with the approach of a sighted person. I tried to feel the center crease but it soon lost itself over the edge of the bed. Then a further thought struck me—a "center" is the middle point, and that being true, there should be as much sheet on one side as the other. From then on it was easy—I merely equalized the drop at the sides and at the top and bottom. The sheet had now smoothed itself. A tight tucking-in and the job was shipshape.

By the time I had finished making our beds and tidying up the dressers I was fatigued almost to the point of exhaustion. This could not, I felt, be due to the physical exertion which actually was negligible. It must be the unaccustomed mental effort now involved. Every step of the procedure had to be projected in my mind and then painstakingly followed through. There was nothing at all automatic about any of it. Could I hope ever to approach normal living again—to orient myself to this molelike existence? The thought of years of change-over and frustration turned me a little sick.

I sat down in one of the easy chairs and gave up to discouragement. Was I beguiling myself into thinking I had come any distance at all on the journey from the Dark Place—what actually was the extent, the permanence of the few things I had essayed to do? At this moment it all looked very futile. Had I set out on a journey that was too extensive for both my physical and my spiritual strength—was I after all a weakling at core? I let myself wallow in such thinking until quietly, unobtrusively, the little flame shone into my consciousness. Was I going to snuff out its clear shining in this mire of despair? I pulled myself up. "No," I said aloud and gave the beds a little kick. I went to another part of the house where I reported to Clyde that I had just conquered a couple of beds. As usual, this positive affirmation was pure alchemy—the negative gloom disappeared and warm assurance took its place.

On the days that Mazie was not with us I attended to many other household chores. I found I could dust very thoroughly through the sense of touch. I could brush lampshades, plump cushions, water plants, and in general keep the rooms looking as we liked them. I ran into a small snarl when I tried to tidy the magazines. We keep magazines on a long low table and we like them neatly arranged for convenience as well as appearance. A sighted person can effect such an arrangement without thought, even while carrying on a conversation. But blind, I can not tell back from front, top from bottom. My tidying efforts in this area resulted in a patchwork effect such as a three-year-old might achieve. One day my inquisitive fingers discovered that all the magazines on the table were put together in the same way. My clue was the metal staple hiding under the sleek paper cover. That staple, like a lot of the world today, puts up a smooth front but at the back he proves surprising rough, even jagged. I was delighted, for from now on all I needed to do was slide my fingers quickly along the magazine's spine, feel for the telltale staple and know at once which was the front side. From that I could easily determine the top and bottom. My joy at this small triumph, however, was short lived. The next day the postman delivered two magazines which utterly demolished my fine system —one of them had the rough side of the staple on the front, the other was stapled from the inside straight through all the pages. Only then did the simple and unfailing solution to this problem come to me—to turn down the upper corner of the back cover of every magazine when it first arrives. With this uniform identification I am now the equal of a sighted person in this area.

The life of a blind person—indeed of any handicapped person —is bedeviled not only by the large tragic things—sometimes I feel these are the most bearable—but by innumerable small bedevilments that irritate and annoy like so many buzzing, stinging insects, biting and inflaming without letup, without hope of relief.

I worked very hard at arranging table appointments for meals. I am sure that at first the results were more than a little tipsy looking, but I gradually improved. At least the silver paralleled the sides of the mats and napkins and tumblers no longer huddled in confusion near the center.

In all these activities I had some nasty experiences with tipping over vases of flowers and the consequent mopping up, with sending ashtrays crashing. Little by little I learned to "sneak" up on objects thus avoiding much of this upsetting. I learned to approach everything with the back of my hand rather than reaching out with my finger tips first. Why this is a safer approach I do not know even now but it is a good tip for sighted persons who might have to search for something in the dark. I have formed the habit, too, of letting my left hand serve as a kind of escort for my right, letting it guard and guide whatever the right hand may be doing.

There are innumerable small things that hamper a handicapped person. Take the episode of the button that had just popped off my husband's shirt—the very shirt, of course, that he wanted to wear this very evening. But why should that be disturbing? A mere shirt button? Pooh! I had replaced dozens of such in my life. Hand me the shirt, and the button. Feeling very confident, I brought out my small sewing basket and immediately was struck by the unfamiliar feel of its fittings. I knew I could, with the aid of a small gadget I had been given, thread a needle, but which was the white thread? I had to ask help on that. Later I learned to notch spools for color identification. Getting that button sewed on was a dismaying experience. I seemed to make no headway at all. I would not have believed that four small holes in one small button could be so elusive. The thread looped around, over, and under my needle and, in thrusting the needle into a hole which I had by some miracle located, I either sewed twice through that hole or skipped it altogether. The most I can say for that initial attempt is that it held for one wearing and then I really set to work to learn what I thought I already knew. Today, whenever I hear someone boasting, "Oh, I could do that with my eyes shut," I am inclined to lift an eyebrow. I used to say that too, but a shirt button made me eat my words.

During these busy weeks of our settling in I continued the arduous business of increasing my ease at table. I was sharply aware that sooner or later Clyde and I must quit the cloistered existence we had been living, and go about among people again.

We began by going out to restaurants. Since we knew no one in the town there was a comfortable kind of privacy in this anonymity. From the very outset I was confronted by the strange feel of the table appointments. I can not take these in at a glance as sighted persons can. I must establish quietly, smoothly, with the back of my fingers, the exact location of the goblet or tumbler, the coffee cup, the salad or bread-and-butter plate. Table silver is a further consideration and sighted persons rarely realize the difference there is in the balance of a fork, a spoon, even a butter knife. The bowls of spoons, for instance, vary widely in their depth, their flare. I often dine at a place where the soup spoons are so shallow that in my desire to keep them from dripping, I seldom get more than a thimbleful of soup at a dip. Some forks have a well-defined curve to the tines and these are a joy to use but others are so flat in contour that often I can scarcely distinguish between the back and the front. I early learned that all knives—that is, all I have so far encountered—run completely straight along their backbone but their cutting edge juts out. These things may seem such trifles to the sighted that they may wonder why I even mention them but they serve to show, I think, how alert I must be to every circumstance.

The wide variety of restaurant food gave me the opportunity to develop skill with the hard-to-manage items. Little by little I gained greater, more comfortable mastery over everything. One learns to be wary about certain foods—scrambled eggs, for instance, are very elusive—they will disintegrate even after accepting a lift on your fork. Noodle soup is downright fugitive, sliced pineapple is stubborn, and gelatine, whether salad or dessert, will take a nosedive off your fork or spoon unless you are constantly on guard. Fish, of which I am extremely fond, confused me for a long while—not the factor of bones for these were always removed for me—but because what I had heretofore regarded as necessary accompaniments to the serving of fish—the lemon wedges, the tartar or other sauce, the parsley sprig—were now an annoying clutter on my plate. All in all, it was like crossing the equivalent of a barbed-wire entanglement every time I ate fish.

There was something almost ludicrous in this endless striving to accomplish so primal a thing as the appeasement of hunger. All too often during the course of a meal, I would lay down my fork in complete exhaustion, wondering if even such delicious food was worth the effort it was costing me to enjoy it. Many times I had eaten only half of what I really wanted when this weariness would overcome me. Prolonged dawdling was no help, for after a while the food loses its palatability and the waiter his patience. Yet, laborious as it all was, I persevered and there came a time when I began to feel comfortable and at ease. I may not have become a model of grace but I had attained a certain efficiency.

It was after weeks of this restaurant dining that Clyde read in the local paper of a large charity dinner to be given shortly.

"I think we should go," he said. "It will be about the same as a restaurant—the people will all be strangers. You need feel no nervousness. In fact, I think this will be the ideal way for you to take the next step."

I did not permit myself to think much about the affair in advance, but when I came into the great hall and heard all the chatter and laughter my only impulse was to turn around and run home. But I checked this impulse when I heard the note of eager anticipation in Clyde's voice as he said, "Oh, I think this is going to be great fun."

We were the first to be seated at our table, a large one. As the other places filled we found our table companions to be charming, congenial persons with tastes and backgrounds similar to our own. The conversation ranged from Giotto to Picasso, from Chaucer to T. S. Eliot, from Finland to Burma. We enjoyed every moment. As we rose to leave at the end of the dinner, several of these delightful people lingered to say a few last words to us and to assure us of a welcome to this new home. It was then that Clyde reached down and drew from beneath my chair my stout white cane and put it into my hand. Our new acquaintances gasped and, almost as one person, exclaimed,

"Oh, I did not know—I never dreamed—"

"That I am blind?" I finished for them. "It need make no difference, you know."

"But," they went on, still astonished, "no one would ever suspect—you managed the food, there never was any hesitation—you always looked directly at the person with whom you were conversing. Are you completely without sight?"

"Quite," I had to tell them.

We went home that night—Clyde and I—happier than we had been in months. What these kind, new friends did not know was that this was my first dinner party since I had lost my sight and we had come, more than a little fearful, of how I would meet this challenge. We were mightily encouraged, for the test had been made among complete strangers—not among old friends who might excuse or condone any lapse or mistake. It was even more than this. It showed us clearly that the stand I had taken months earlier was tenable—that I must never permit this blindness to set me apart from other people nor to impose inactivity upon me.

For days after this I went about with a veritable glockenspiel chiming in my heart, not only for myself but as well for the lift this pleasant experience had brought to my husband. I was so elated, in fact, that I gladly accepted his suggestion, a few weeks later, that we go to another dinner, also a public affair, honoring a distinguished visitor in town. This proved no less enjoyable as to delightful tablemates, but its real value to me lay in the fact that on this occasion I had the salutary experience of a personal "Waterloo."

After the usual fruit cup, I was appalled to have an enormous Cornish hen plopped down before me. I explored its size with the tines of my fork—it was unquestionably the largest I had ever measured. Heretofore I had encountered this kind of bird in a more or less manageable size—in what might be called a "junior miss" size—and I was terrified at the prospect of dismembering this outsize model.

What was even worse was the fact that this bird was served on the world's smallest dinner plate, and, crowded close, were sweet potatoes, rice and asparagus. I knew I was whipped—I declined to attack it. The complaints of my neighbors struggling with their equally huge birds confirmed me in my decision. A thoughtful waiter finally removed my plate to a side table and carved off a few slices for me and so I thus came off better than the others. It was a good experience for I felt I now had faced the ultimate in gastronomic obstacles. Hereafter, I thought, they would at least be of lesser size.

As time went on and we made friends in the community, we began to receive dinner invitations which we happily accepted.

Dinner parties were always my delight—they still are. As far as I know, my friends do not alter their menus to make things easier for me—I hope they do not. I never feel the need of apologizing for eating a bit more slowly than the others. To eat slowly gives me a greater sense of sureness and that tends to reduce others' concern about me. Actually it would do them all good to eat at my pace—this would also give us more time for good talk.

One form of activity which I postponed as long as possible was shopping for my own personal needs. After years of familiarity with the New York shops I found myself backing away from the idea of learning the local stores. Eventually it had to be done and in actuality it proved relatively simple. At the outset I always inform the salesperson that I am blind and tell them as clearly as possible what I am looking for. They go to great pains to help me. They make the extra effort of putting merchandise, whenever possible, into my hands so that I may feel the size, the texture, the form. Whenever the factor of color enters into a purchase I try to take with me something from my sighted days, something whose color I remember clearly—a belt, a scarf, even a sweater. Then by asking, "Is what you are showing me up or down the color scale from this sample?" I can gain some idea of what I am being offered. I know, of course, that nothing can be exactly as I picture it but I also know that the store people and my friends try very hard to help me find what I have in mind. Hosiery shades, whose names grow more elusive with each season, seem the most difficult for salesgirls to describe and for me to comprehend.

I shall never forget the sensitive tact of one saleswoman. She had shown me several articles but I was unable at the time to make a decision and said I would telephone her later. Next day when I called her to order the one I had decided upon, she said,

"Oh, yes, I remember you very well. Your husband was with you." A less sensitive person, in identifying me, would have blurted out, "Oh, yes—you can't see," or "You are the blind one." In all my shopping expeditions I have known nothing but kindness except in one instance. This occurred in the shop of a tailor who was fitting a suit for me. When I firmly refused to give in on one detail, he burst out impatiently, "Oh, why should you care—you can't see it anyway." I reminded him that my husband and friends could see it and I like them to be pleased. I let him finish the work but, unwilling to risk a repetition of such an incident, I have never returned to his shop. He is a good tailor, too.

I must admit that there is one area of shopping that continues to be an ordeal by fire. This is in the selection of hats. Hats were always a great passion with me and now, not to know what my headgear looks like from even one side, much less from "all round" is as near to heartbreak as a woman can come. Today I must depend on luck or my friends, neither of which, I confess, I would have trusted before. I often wonder what I look like in these new hats.

An odd thing happens every time I shop for a hat. As the sales-girl adjusts the hat, I instinctively reach out for the hand mirror that always lies on the little table. (This habit goes very deep with every woman.) Each time I must remind myself sharply that mirrors—all mirrors—are now but a part of that other life I once lived. I always loved them so—large or small, they bring such sparkle to a room, whether it is in a home, a restaurant, or a great opera house. Mirrors always prod us into looking our best and reward us, smile for smile.

I continue to miss mirrors from my life—their influence, their help. Aside from their esthetic lift they are practical. I no longer have the comfort, the satisfaction, of that last look into the mirror when I am dressed for an occasion. Everybody knows the importance of that final "once-over." Not being able to do this has given me trouble more than once. One evening, after seating ourselves at a symphony concert, Clyde suddenly noticed that I was still wearing several clamps in my hair. On another occasion, as we were driving to a luncheon, he said, "You know, your hat looks so different from what it did when you first bought it." Since this was only the second or third time I had worn the hat, I could not believe it was showing wear and tear. I ran an exploratory finger about the brim. Oops!—I had put that docile hat on backwards. If I had had a last look in some mirror, these incidents and many others would not have happened. The outcome of all this has been that I now stand for a minute inspection before going out—an inspection almost as detailed as one of those white-gloved military ordeals. So far this has worked very well and is worth the few minutes required for it. With this precautionary measure, I need never fear a repetition of something which happened to me several years ago.

Just before I became blind I did something which I had never done before and certainly never shall do again. I went into my favorite shoe shop for a pair of navy calf pumps. I was so delighted with what the salesman showed me that he, knowing the difficulty I have about lasts, suggested that I buy the same shoe in another color. It ended by my buying a red and a brown pair as well as the navy. It was a fine idea for me as a sighted person but as a blind woman I realized, as I arranged my closet, that the identical "feel" of these shoes might prove troublesome. So I had placed these three pairs at the end of the long shoe rack, setting them in alphabetic order—brown, navy, red. I was to learn later that my system was fallible.

One day Mazie, who is the embodiment of thoughtfulness, decided she would "brush up" my shoes as she was cleaning the closet. Not knowing about my alphabet, she restored the shoes to the rack according to her own idea of color arrangement and went about her business. A day or so later, when I was hurriedly dressing, I went with confidence to the rack, stepped into what I had every reason to believe were brown shoes and rushed out to be taken to an appointment at the dentist's. As I sat waiting my turn I felt a real pleasure in having selected the brown woollen dress and the brown shoes on this early fall day. It must be remembered that I, like other blind persons, cannot while away the time in waiting rooms by riffling through magazines. I am limited to my own thoughts, to listening to the sighs of my fellow patients or to the monotonous rhythm of the aerating mechanism of the tropical fish tank. The good doctor had thought to provide diversion for his patients with this tank of bright-colored fish but to me it is only a snuffling noise. When the assistant came to take me in to the dentist she whispered,

"Mrs. McCoy, did you know you have on shoes of different colors? It does not matter here, but I thought you would want to know in case you are going on somewhere else."

Luckily I was not, but the bite of the dentist's drill was a fitting acompaniment to my malediction on those shoes.

That was not the end of the story, however. Months later, as I was telling this as an amusing joke on myself, one woman in the group spoke up.

"I did not know you at that time Mrs. McCoy, but I, too, was in that waiting room on that day and I was simply fascinated by your shoes. I wondered if you might be a style expert with a flair for starting new fashions, for the combination of one navy and one red shoe with your brown dress was arresting. When you stop to think about it, why should our shoes always be mated in color?"

Why indeed—except that they always have been. One thing still puzzles me—by what capricious fate was I led to put my right foot into a red shoe, my left into a navy when the odds, one would guess, would be to get two rights or two lefts, thereby warning me immediately of a mistake. Today, everything is quiet in the shoe department—except for one thing, scuffs. I wish I could invent a sturdy, but chic, little bumper for my heels, for the risers of stone and concrete steps are cruelly abrasive.

It is incredible what sightless persons must provide for, must seek to forestall. We must be acutely aware every moment, must think out every detail of our life, for we dare not leave anything to chance. Such necessity was forcefully, and surprisingly, brought home to us one busy morning.

We had been working for several hours in our small garden when we discovered that we were running shorts of plants and fertilizer. Without considering how we looked, we hopped into the car and drove to a garden supply establishment. Clyde was wearing baggy slacks, a sagging sweater, and a battered old beret. I had on a calico squaw-dress bought in Arizona and a Chinese garden hat. As we waited just inside the store, a salesman came up to us and, in a brisk manner, said, "Good morning—I am very sorry but we cannot help you today. Perhaps some other time—" With that he ushered us out to the sidewalk and returned inside.

"How did he know what we wanted?" I asked in surprise. It had all happened so suddenly, I was confused.

"He didn't," Clyde said, sounding equally puzzled. Then he began to laugh.

"I don't understand—" I began.

"That's because you don't see what we look like," he was laughing uproariously now. "My dear, that man thought we were beggars—a woman with a white cane, led by a sighted friend, making the rounds. It was a natural mistake. Come on, we're going back in there."

We went back and, with explanations and apologies, the outcome was pleasant enough but the incident taught me a lesson. From that day on I began to break a rule I had followed all my adult life—that of choosing to be underdressed rather than risking being overdressed. Now, shopping as a blind woman, I dress "to the nines." In fact, I am conscious of being a little too dressy much of the time but I feel this is safer for my morale.

My morale, I must confess, needed frequent bolstering during these weeks and months of struggle. Sometimes, when I was tempted toward discouragement and surrender, I would energize myself by humming an old Czech folk song which I had known for a long time—*Plow your land, my son.* This song is well-beloved by all the Czech people, a kind of bond between them. I recall the newspapers' poignant reporting of Jan Masaryk's funeral when the elderly Benes wept openly as a children's chorus sang, "Plow your land, my son." The song's implication for me was clear and powerful and I never failed to respond to its admonition.

In all this "plowing of the land" of my blindness—the learning of new ways of living—I had the invaluable companionship of a fellow-learner, Butch, my parakeet. While he strove to master phrases, I struggled to master the problems of the handicapped. I taught him the phrases but he taught me, by his tireless efforts and his dogged determination, to persevere in my own endeavors. His persistence in bringing every word into assonance with the pattern I set for him was an example I could not ignore, a challenge I could not refuse.

Butch learned some twenty-odd phrases—certainly not a record number—but he had the waggish knack of introducing them at the most telling points. For instance, if I were disappointed about something or other he would fly to my shoulder and say, wisely and soothingly, *"C'est la vie."* It was so pat I could not resist laughing aloud and thus was restored to a livelier mood. To be sure, he mixed things up at times, being very likely to greet you on a hot July day with a joyous "Merry Christmas" or he might prove embarrassing by asking crisply, "What time is it?" when a guest had stayed overlong. To me he was always captivating, no matter what he said.

I recall one day, however, when we both got our "come-uppance." A handyman was doing some minor repairs in the house and Butch, in a fit of generosity, ran through his whole repertory —"Birds can talk," "You rapscallion," "God bless you," "Don't be silly,"—and all the rest. My heart swelled with something like maternal pride and I could not resist exclaiming, "Isn't he wonderful!" Without interrupting his work the man replied,

"He's all right, I guess—but you ought to hear my wife's parakeet say, "Pretty bird."

Abruptly Butch stopped talking—it was as if someone had turned off a switch. Was he, by this silence, rebuking me for having failed to teach him so dainty a morsel as "pretty bird" or had he decided not to waste his talent on so unappreciative an audience? Whatever the reason, he was stonily silent for the rest of the time the workman was there. As he was leaving, the man said,

"Maybe your bird needs some special tonic. He don't seem to talk much, does he?"

71

"Not too," I told him, resorting to a popular localism.

Butch always made me feel that I was important to him, that I still counted in the world. In some subtle way, he seemed to sense that I was different from other people—physically not quite their equal. He was often a rowdy rascal with my husband, teasing him and nipping sharply at him but whenever he came to my shoulder, he was gentleness itself, speaking words with something like affectionate concern.

Through my association with Butch I learned afresh that all we send into the lives of others comes back into our own, for the words and phrases with which he regaled me, cheered and strengthened me, were precisely—in intonation and inflection— the phrases I had taught to him—word for word, syllable by syllable.

Another companionship entered my life soon after we had settled into our new home. It came like a full-rigged ship, laden low with rich treasure, and all of it mine to revel in. It was the Talking Book.

Since the beginning of blindness I had missed reading. To be sure, much was read to me, but this always involved the fitting together of two persons' time. I was often desolated by the great yearning to read—independently, privately.

For years I had known, in a vague sort of way, of the Talking Books but it was only after a New York friend, knowing my lifelong devotion to reading, suggested that these books might go a long way toward filling my need, that I began to think of them for myself.

I made inquiry of the regional branch of the Talking Book Library for the Blind and they sent me the proper application blanks. One of these had to be taken to an ophthalmologist who examined my eyes and attested his findings on the blank. This established my status as a legally blind person. When these blanks had been returned to the Library I received an unbelievably long list of books on which I was to check fifty as a starter list. From this list they would send me books as they became available. I was overwhelmed.

For any of my readers who may not know about the Talking Books, let me pause a moment to tell something about them. Established in 1934 by an Act of Congress, it is a service which provides, free of charge, to any blind person in the United States, the blessing of independent reading. This service, under the supervision of the Library of Congress, is now taken advantage of by several hundred thousand blind people in our country. The Talking Book is a recording of reading matter—books, plays, poetry and so forth—on long-playing phonograph records. These look exactly like other records except that the title appears in Braille on the first side on each disc. For distribution to readers these records are packed and sent by mail in sturdy cases, strapped and labeled. The Post Office Department transports these cases without charge to and from the blind reader.

The range of this reading material is limitless—there being about four thousand titles on the full list. One may choose fiction, biography, history, philosophy, science, religious works, Westerns, whodunits. The length of the book, of course, determines the number of records used. There are a few works which need only one record—at the other extreme being works that require well over a hundred. Mr. Churchill's *Second World War*, for instance, is recorded on 105 records and the combined recordings of various sections of the Bible run well above that figure. An average novel requires fewer than twenty records but that very un-average novel *Gone With the Wind* fills seventy-two records. Each side of these records takes approximately twenty-five minutes to play.

Bimonthly lists of new recordings are sent to readers and this is the counterpart of going into a bookshop and browsing among the new titles. I find I must hold a tight rein on myself in checking off my choices or, before I realize it, I will have asked for more than I can conveniently find time for. In the beginning the Library sent me four or five books at a time. Many readers, I am told, can move through such a number at a pace comparable to that of a mowing machine streaking through an expanse of grass. With my other interests, however, I soon found that I could not keep up with such a mass of reading matter, pleasant though such a pastime might be. Having so many books in the house gave me an uncomfortable feeling of pressure for I kept thinking of other blind persons who might be waiting for the very books that were idling under my roof. I learned that a reader has the privilege of stipulating when and how many books shall be sent to him. I finally determined that two books at a time were a comfortable number for me, so I requested that two books be sent to me and that only upon their return to the Library should two others be sent.

This has proved a very happy arrangement and for several years these wonderful companions have traveled to and from my house in pairs, much in the manner of policemen or nuns. I must add that often they are very mixed pairs, amusingly mixed at times. For example, *Madame de Pompadour* arrived with *The Gay Monarch,* who proved to be, not Louis XV as one would expect, but Edward VII. On another day *The Brave Bulls* reached our door with *Ninety Dozen Glasses*—surely not the proverbial china shop bulls, for not one glass was broken. Such laughable combinations do not occur with every delivery but often enough to pique my curiosity. I think the high mark came on the day when I welcomed the postman at the door and he asked with a chuckle,

"Starting a circus?"

In one hand he held the strap of *The Leopard*—in the other hand the strap of *The Red Pony*.

What really brings these books alive is the quality of the reading. There is no hit-or-miss selection of readers—there is never any droning on, no unimaginative mere calling off of words. The Talking Book readers, both men and women, are experts. The majority of them are professional actors or actresses who know how to interpret—vitally—what they read. The voice is invariably the right one for the content of the book. There is artistry in every recording, amazing nuances of voice, delicate shadings of emotion. It is almost impossible to describe the excellence of these readings.

My pleasure in listening to these recordings is surpassed only by my gratitude for them. Interesting, thought provoking, informing—they are for me both stimulating and relaxing. There is an added quality of theater in these books. With each bundle of books, adventure comes into this house—and I experience sharp anticipation of what will emerge from their magic insides. Even when I give myself the pleasure of rereading books which I enjoyed years before, I have the tingling certainty that they are going to have more meaning for me as read by these artists than when I read them to myself. They have a fresh and lively impact —these rereadings—even when one knows "how the end comes out."

My enthusiasm for the Talking Book knows no bounds nor can I say enough in praise of the manner in which this service is handled. I am enormously grateful to the Librarian and her staff—

four-fifths of them are volunteers, bless them—for their warm interest, their immediate and helpful response to inquiries and requests.

To round out the list of those to whom I am indebted for this great boon is our young suburban mail carrier. We listen for the heavy rumble of his truck whenever I am expecting new books and go out to our mail box to take them from him. Sometimes, however, we do not hear his approach and then, quite unexpectedly, he is at our door with the heavy bundles and a cheery greeting. He is wonderful—may his kind increase.

CHAPTER 6

The Nadir

LITTLE by little our life had become a pleasant routine with occasional surprises to give peaks to the graph. We had made friends with many congenial individuals and groups, especially among the university people, from the president at the center to the young instructors on the outer rim of the academic circle, with all the subtle and consequential gradations of deans and professors in between. A remarkable aspect of all this is that our acquaintance covers so many age groups.

The fine library at the university has become an important part of our life, its director and staff cordial and helpful in dozens of ways. The same has been true of the departments of Music, Art, English, the Humanities—not forgetting our friends in Horticulture.

I was indescribably grateful that I had been enabled to master many of the mechanics of a blind person's life. In all of this, perforce, I was self-taught for I had had no one to teach me the best-by-test ways, nor to point out any short cuts. I had had to learn everything through trial and error. Nevertheless, the encouraging results of my effort and perseverance led me to believe that I had come some distance on my journey.

As time went on, however, I began to sense that something was troubling me—something far below the surface probably, but the Geiger counter of my mind was picking it up. It was a kind of unrest growing within me, an anxious questioning, a distinct feeling of unfulfillment. Was there not something further toward which I should be pressing?

Everyone about me seemed to be enlarging the area of his usefulness, of his knowledge, his endeavor. In contrast, I appeared to have come to a halt and I felt strongly that I should plan to widen the scope of my own activities. This was quite like the feeling I had had during my early years in New York when I had decided that my life should be more than a mere round of pleasure.

There was this difference—when I went to New York I carried with me a pattern of life which I could more or less follow. Now I had no pattern suitable for this darkness—no clear idea of what I wished to do—of what, in fact, I might be able to do. So far, my feeling was only a vague, unfocussed reaching-out and I wanted to turn it to something distinct, definite. I came to realize that I needed expert guidance and we began to make inquiries.

We learned that the State School for the Blind, located in another town, did not enroll adults but a short time later a representative of the State Council for the Blind called at our house.

We welcomed him and the three of us settled ourselves comfortably in the sunroom. I asked the caller,

"Do you have something special you wish to talk to me about?"

"No—no, I was given your name and I am just checking with you. I get to this town several times a year."

"I am so glad that you have come," I told him. "I am sure you have had much experience in guiding people and that you can help me a great deal. I am very new-blind, you know."

"No—I did not know."

I went on to tell him that I had always filled my days with activity and that I hoped to find ways to continue to do this in spite of the blindness. I said I had heard of wonderful methods by which the blind could learn to use their old skills or to learn new ones. I had, in particular, been told that blind persons could attend some kind of training course where they learn to manage their housekeeping efficiently in ways specially contrived for the blind. I should so like to hear of anything, I told him further, that might open a door to me for self-discovery in my new state.

"Well, what is it you want?" he asked gruffly.

"I suppose that what I am really reaching out for is, briefly, Occupation."

"My goodness," he exclaimed, "with a nice house like this I wouldn't think you'd need work."

"I probably did not make myself clear," I apologized, more than a little taken aback. What I mean is occupation of my time, my efforts, using my energy and whatever resources I have. The blind, like other persons, have twenty-four hours in every day and many of us have limitless energy. How can a blind person use all this to count for something?"

"Well, what do you want to know?"

I began to wonder at just what level I could communicate with this man.

"Could I join one of those housekeeping classes?" I ventured.

He almost exploded with impatience. "No!" he stated emphatically. "You are too old—we won't fool with anybody over forty."

Inasmuch as I never think of myself as being hopelessly gerontal, this struck me rather hard, but I decided to ignore his lack of suavity, of understanding.

"Many people do their best work after reaching forty," I reminded him. "Is it quite fair to consider chronological age when one has the desire to be active?"

"Desire? Lots of people hanker to do things they have no equipment for," he told me pontifically. On that score I could have expressed complete agreement with him, but I merely said,

"In the natural course of events I have more than a score of years—active years—ahead of me. I am a strong and energetic person and I feel an obligation to fill these years with something other than bemoaning my bad luck in becoming blind. What, now, would you suggest for me?"

Without the slightest hesitation he told me, "Now, then, if you are so set on doing something, I'll tell you exactly what to do. I've had lots of experience and I know what fits each person."

Then he really got down to business. "You go down to the five-and-dime, and buy yourself one of those little weaving frames—it won't cost you much. Then you buy whatever material and colors they tell you to buy, and then you weave up some pot holders. It will take you some time because you are going to find that your fingers don't manage as well as they did in your twenties."

I really could not believe I was hearing aright. I flexed my fingers—they could still do keyboard exercises at high speed with the metronome but he was prophesying that they would be clumsy and slow on the little weaving frame.

He went on: "Now, then, when you get a few done, sell them to your friends. You might get as much as a quarter a piece for them. After that, make up some more and then get somebody as your guide and go from house to house selling them. You won't find many people that will turn down a blind woman selling something."

Keeping my tone as smooth as I could, I questioned, "In other words, you think that this is the best thing for me, considering my experience and background."

"Your background means nothing now." He brushed along, "Now, then, you said you wanted to learn something about keeping your house clean. (Actually I had asked him only about household management.) I'll give you a good tip about that, too. When you mop your floors, I'll bet lots of times you wonder if you get them clean. Well, here's how you can tell. Take off your shoes and stockings and walk across the floor in your bare feet— I imagine your feet are still sensitive—and you'll soon find the grit you missed. I picked up that trick from a colored lady—she's blind, too, and likes to keep her house nice. And believe you me, she sells lots of those pot holders."

"May the good Lord bless her mightily," was all I could say.

The "counsellor" went pompously on. "Now, then, before I write up my report, I want to know when you'll start making some of those pot holders."

"Oh, I hope not for a long time," I told him in complete honesty.

I heard him catch his breath in vexation. "Think yourself

81

above something like that, eh? You asked for my advice. You know, you remind me exactly of a fellow I had on my list a while back. He went blind suddenly and he couldn't bear to be idle— said he had to be doing something. So I fixed him up with a neat little job—night work in connection with the railroad. And he kept griping to me that he had his Ph.D. and should be doing something at his own level. Now what do you think of that?"

"Frankly, I think the man was right," I managed to say. "Apparently he found no challenge in that work—it was not what he meant when he said he wanted something to do. Moreover, when you gave this job to him you took it away from some man who might not be able to work at any other level."

"Now, let me tell you something else," he began.

At this point I heard my husband, who never enters a conversation he feels belongs to others, clear his throat and say,

"It was very good of you to make this call, but I think you must excuse us now."

I heard hackles in the tone of his voice. There are hackles in a voice as truly as there are hackles on a dog's neck and I knew his were rising. I then heard him leave his chair and move toward the front door and I heard the man follow him.

"Thank you for coming," Clyde said, "but I think there is no need for further calls. Good day."

Our caller went out to his car which was parked in our driveway and sat there dictating into a machine for a long time— enough time, in fact, to have described everything in our house.

Clyde came back to the sunroom. I was beaten down, speechless. I was not angry at the man's ineptitude, but I was truly bewildered. This person patently had no idea that there was any kind of help, other than financial, that people reach out for. He had manifested no interest in my background nor in any special

82

training or experience I might have had. He had made no suggestion of any IQ or aptitude tests.

Clyde, sensing my mood, said with true masculine brevity, "Oh, forget about him. You don't have to see him again—ever."

"But think of those who must," I murmured.

I could not fully throw off the discouragement his visit had built up, although I reminded myself that discouragement is a thief—of our time, our energy, our hope. He could have lifted my morale immeasurably with even one encouraging phrase. Instead, he had with his blunt, knuckle-hard phrases thrust me a long way back in the direction of the Dark Place. He had spelled out—and not subtly—my present situation, that of a handicapped person—inconsequential, negligible.

I have tried to rationalize this man's behavior on the ground that he probably could not envision me as potentially employable. The accent today—and probably rightly—is to place people in jobs. An impressive number of people placed in jobs is a tangible thing to put on a report sheet. Perhaps the day will come when all blind persons—whether or not they can or need work—may avail themselves of rehabilitation for independent living.

Under ordinary circumstances, I would in a short time have cast off this gloom and doubt—would have seen the whole matter in its true perspective—but I was very new in this kind of life. My footing on the path was infirm, my sense of direction not well established. Even so, I am sure I would have dispelled earlier the feeling of exile which moved like a dark shadow above me for days had it not been for a second incident which followed close upon the heels of the counsellor's visit.

An election day came along shortly afterward and it never occurred to me that there might be any special trial in connection with so familiar a routine as voting. From the beginning of blindness I had endeavored to lead, if only in a fumbling manner, a normal life—to carry on whatever activities were still open to me. I have a certain sense of civic responsibility and I regard the right to vote as both a privilege and a duty. This special election was being held to settle some controversial local questions and there was considerable "feeling" about them in the community.

Clyde and I went to the polling place—a school house—at an hour when we thought there would be a lull in the voting, not when it would be brisk. This should make things easier not only for us but for the attendants. When we arrived there was only a short waiting line. After we had established that we were properly registered and thus entitled to vote, we were handed slips to sign. A woman spoke to Clyde,

"I'll take care of her," meaning me. "You go to the next table to fill in your slip."

She seemed to be a very large woman and reeked of stale perfume. She thrust a pencil between my fingers and then, with fat, perspiring pressure, squashed my hand down on the paper, all the while shouting as if I could not hear, "Now just make your mark —right there—make your mark."

"My what?" I asked, incredulous.

"Your mark—your mark. You're blind, ain't you?" For emphasis she gave my fingers another thump.

"Yes, I am blind," I admitted, "but isn't it customary for people to sign their names?"

"Oh, yes, of course, people do but you just make a mark."

Quickly, quietly, I drew from my coat pocket the open metal rectangle which I use in writing my signature. I laid it on the paper and without a word I crisply wrote my name, all three parts of it.

84

"I wouldn't ha' believed it," panted the big woman.

"That is all right," I assured her, "but will you do me a favor? The next time you deal with a handicapped person, please do not add to his load by assuming that he is also a moron."

Clyde joined me and we moved toward the voting machine. An attendant snatched the slip from my hand and shouted in a voice readily heard in any corner of the school hall.

"All right, I'll attend to this for you. How do you want to vote on the first proposal—'for' or 'against'?"

I was astonished. "Just a moment," I said, "isn't there still in this country of ours something called a secret vote?"

"Secret vote? Oh, yes—but you just tell me what you want here—'for' or 'against.' I'll push down the little tab. Tell me now. Let's not delay."

"I am sorry," I said, "but I'm still on this question of the secret vote. Do other people call out their preference in this fashion?"

"Of course, people do not, but you are not"—she hesitated, as if groping for the word, "You are not—not—" she found the word and flung it at me, "You are not competent."

There it was—laid right on the line for me, and I did not like it. In fact, I was indignant, not only for myself but for all the handicapped.

"Please," I begged, "all this shouting is very humiliating to me. I am neither deaf nor illiterate, you know—only blind. Don't you think that I might at least be accorded the courtesy of whispered questions?"

She lowered her voice a fraction of a decibel but maintained her impatience. "Come on—let's get going—'for' or 'against'?" This had become her theme song.

I tried a new tack. "How would this be?" I ventured, tentatively. "My husband knows exactly how I wish to vote. He can

85

go into the booth with me, move the little tabs for me and I myself can move the big lever. That would give me my secret vote —right?"

I could hear her speaking in an undertone to several persons— probably co-workers. She came out of the conversational huddle, however, with a firm,

"No, that would be impossible. The rule is that there can be only one person at a time in the booth."

I could understand their decision—some of them were watchers at the polls, and there are always watchers watching watchers —and how could they gauge where such a thing might end? The woman's voice now returned to its full booming as she proclaimed,

"Only one person in the booth, and you can't manage by yourself. Now, make your decision."

After a moment, I made my decision. "Would you be so good as to give me the slip I signed?" She thrust it into my hand.

"This has been a very harsh experience for me," I said, tearing the slip into bits. "Just because I have been deprived of my sight, I am now deprived of one of my rights as a first-class citizen— the secret vote. As a protest against such unfair treatment, I am declining to vote. I believe I am doing something real for democracy in taking this stand."

My husband, who regards a question like this as a very personal and private one, was in complete agreement with my attitude and decision and, after he had voted, we went home.

By the time of the next election our polling place had been shifted and my special problem recognized. Nowadays the "gals" at the new place make voting a really pleasant experience for me, but I shall never forget what that first ordeal did to me.

For what it did—and in the most cruel way—was to plunge me again into despair—despair as dismal as what I had felt in the early period of blindness, because since emigrating from that fearsome locale, I had had an interlude of elation over my progress and had enjoyed during this interim release from much of the pressure of gloom. The sudden drop from the level of elation to this lower stratum of discouragement had all but beaten the breath out of my courage. Suppose, I found myself thinking, these people are right—the man from the Blind Council, the women at the voting booth. Have I, through this infliction of blindness, really become incompetent? Am I beyond the age to learn new things? If this be true, I thought, what a life confronts me. Do I have the wit—to say nothing of the will—to surmount these obstacles? I wondered.

Later that evening Clyde and I fell to discussing the plight of all handicapped persons. They seem so walled-off from so-called normal people. Why should this be? Was it due, perhaps, to some oversensitiveness on the part of the handicapped or to the indifference, the lack of understanding, on the part of other people, even their embarrassment in the presence of the abnormal? It might be, we concluded, a bit of both but, whatever it was, the situation constituted unquestionably a kind of exile for any handicapped person. That very day I, myself, had been made to feel this exile keenly—exile not only from the land of color, form, and movement but also from the land of fair and equal consideration. I was very homesick, that election day, for a land I had once known and loved with a great passion—my native land of sight. During the next few days I seemed unable to summon anything from anywhere that would give me the leverage to lift myself out of the funk, the miasma of this dispirited state.

What made these two incidents so difficult for me was that their weight was piled on top of two problems which I had had ever since the beginning of the blindness. These problems were with me always, and although I tried hard to solve them, they had so far eluded solution, even analysis. One of these problems was the sense of loneliness which invaded me. Sometimes it was sharp and stabbing, at other times it was a dull incessant bruising.

For years I had had the conviction that every human being lives his inner life in solitude and in my sighted years occasional solitude had been my retreat, my refuge. I had always welcomed the opportunity to retire to such solitude and had drawn strength and repose from it. But at that time my going there was voluntary and the length of my stay was what I wanted to make it. The solitude of blindness is different—vastly, overpoweringly—different. There is nothing voluntary about it and it is of endless duration. I knew, of course, that this feeling of loneliness was induced by the thick and heavy darkness that perpetually enveloped me, and I tried many avenues in the vain attempt to escape the oppression it tended to establish within me. Strangely enough, the loneliness was often felt most poignantly when I was in the company of friends—I seemed so remote from them, so separate, so excommunicated because of the factor of blindness. This painful circumstance was forcibly brought home to me a few days after the election day incident.

I learned that a regional horse show was to be held in our community and I fell upon the idea that this might prove the very tonic I needed. As in the past, the mere thought of any kind of horse show or exhibition was enough to set my blood to bounding. My love of horses goes back to my childhood when my father owned some fine saddle and harness horses. Although I never developed into an expert horsewoman. I had been taught the fine points to look for, in horse, rider or driver. During the many years in New York I had been an ardent spectator at the great National Horse Show. I attended the sober, workman-like afternoon sessions as well as the brilliant evening performances where beautiful women in superb evening gowns, furs and jewels and the military in full dress vied with the equine beauties in the tanbark ring.

Although I took delight in the perfection and style of the harness turnouts—their smart Edwardian flavor—and although I marveled at the coordination of horse and rider in a dressage interlude, it was the jumpers that provided me with genuine thrills. To watch, breathless, as some splendid, high-strung horse holds himself—"collected"—just for the fraction of a second and then, with all his power and his trained instinct for precision, draws himself over the hurdle, whether hedge or bar, is something to stop the heart. What a sickening sound, however, was the referee's thin, squeaky whistle registering a fault.

I usually sat near the reviewing stand but when someone suggested that I sit, for just one performance, at the other end of the ring, directly above where the horses enter, I followed the suggestion and had an entirely, and excitingly, different viewpoint. To look down, and close at hand, upon these magnificent animals as they charge in, excited, straining, at a point directly beneath one, is to feel that one is entering with them, projected on their thrust, keyed to their quivering tension. However, the emotional strain was too great at this vantage point and after one performance I returned to my accustomed section. The resplendent National was not the only horse show that delighted me. Over the years Clyde and I went to many country horse shows, from some of the Westchester shows to Quaker Hill, and up into the Berkshires. There were also the Long Island shows— the Piping Rock in particular. My beautiful young cousin who rode with the Meadowbrook Hunt had been an expert horsewoman from her early teens and it was always the peak of excitement for me to see her ride up on her big mount, Haile Selassie, to receive another silver bowl.

My interest, however, extended far from these eastern shows. I loved the fun at the Quarter Horse meets in the desert country. To the uninitiated these races seem like no race at all—they are so soon over. But once the fever of this sport gets into the blood, it is well-nigh impossible to rid one's self of it. The principal reason for this is that one does not want to be rid of it. In the dry dusty air of the desert, under a blazing sun, with most of the crowd in levis and plaid shirts, and with the aroma of barbecue and coffee pervading the whole atmosphere, the short fast spurt of a race is a heady thing to be part of. Love of the horse is the same, whether in the open stretches of the desert or in the strict formality of Madison Square Garden.

It was such scenes as these that drifted through my mind as I dressed for the local show, choosing a crisp linen dress and a brimmed hat, for the day was warm and sunny. We were a smallish but congenial party that occupied a box that day. All of us were horse devotees and the excitement that ran through us was more than a flutter. I sat in the rear row, insisting that my friends occupy the forward seats since I could "see with my ears."

From the start I had sensed that the acoustics were poor. To a degree this is true of many outdoor arenas, but here the sounds were not merely muffled, they seemed actually to dissipate themselves into thin air. One of my friends read the first part of the program to me and I strained to catch some identifying sound that would give me a clue to what might be going on in the ring, but there was none. As the show progressed there was, intermittently, a lively round of applause, an occasional small cry of disappointment but there was no sound from the ring to help me construct a picture of what was going on there. A horse show, like a tennis match, is usually quiet, but I had thought I might catch some sound—the creak of fine saddle leather, the puffing of a winded horse, the faint rhythm of hoofs—but nothing came through.

When, once or twice, I ventured to ask what was happening, my friends would reply politely but in such hurried, staccato phrases that I scarcely caught the words. They would say something like, "Oh, that happened so fast, I can't describe it to you," which left me with a complete blank. Or, "I wish you could see how well that girl is doing this," which told me nothing at all except that there were young entrants in this event. Soon realizing that these friends had had no experience in communicating what they saw, I gave up interrupting their pleasure. For at least three-fourths of the show I sat silent, solitary. The feeling of being exiled from those about me deepened and broadened and heightened. My program lay in my lap, crisp and new, useless, a mute reminder of what no longer existed for me. Although it was a warm day I felt chilly for, as never before, I was conscious of the Beast's paws over my eyes and now they seemed not hot but cold and clammy as they pressed hard upon my eyeballs, so that angry sparks and dazzling whorls and streaks of light tormented me.

I shivered. I felt an almost irresistible compulsion to pry loose those icy paws, to tear them away and thus reveal the scene that I knew was so close at hand. This was one of the few times in my blindness I have felt a fierce resentment against my plight. Why, I asked myself, should this thing have happened to me? An inner voice countered, If not to you, then to whom? In all honesty, I could not think of anyone on whom I could have the cruelty to pin this thing.

As I sat there, surrounded by friends and happy onlookers, the old clouds of negative thinking began to gather, to lower. In spirit, I left the horse show at this point. I turned my thoughts within—I began to wonder how I could have slumped down into this depression of spirit when I had known such happiness so short a while ago, during all the time, in fact, that I was learning the rudiments of my blind existence. How could I so soon have forgotten the genuine quality of that happiness? Genuine? Yes—but it must have been what Pascal calls a "feeble happiness," else it would not have withered so soon, and died and disappeared.

Why had I not been more vigilant about my thoughts? I knew that I myself had admitted to my thinking those wretched creatures—self-doubt, fear, pessimism, discouragement, the temptation to surrender. Like Hieronymus Bosch figures, they had sidled up to me, one by one, and I had regarded them with a kind of hypnotic fascination, not consciously accepting them but, before I knew what was happening, they had scooted past my barriers and were all over the place, making themselves at home in my emotions, my thinking, in my very heart. I should have alerted myself when they first began to prowl and skulk about the house of my courage, my perseverance—should have gone out immediately and with my own indignation clubbed them into nothingness. Their usurpation, however, was accomplished so slyly, so nimbly and quietly, that I had not realized what was actually happening. Such infiltration, sadly enough and all too often, occurs in many areas—intellectual, moral, political.

As is my wont in moments of bewilderment, I turned for direction to wiser minds than mine—to what I could recall from the poets, the philosophers, the composers, and from saints and sages. These had never before failed me but now some of their loftiest sentiments and expressions seemed only glib phrases. Something I had not thought of in years rose to the surface—Tchai-kovsky's *None but the lonely heart can know my sorrow*. It should have served to remind me that others down through the ages had borne this sense of loneliness but at this moment it was just a nice old song, of scant help and no comfort.

There was no denying to myself that my funds of courage and persistence were running low—I was disheartened at the very thought of the further striving it would take to live in the world of the sighted. Everything was geared to fit the needs of people who can see.

I did not know at that time what I have since learned, that this phase of heavy discouragement is a common experience of most persons struggling to emerge from a disaster—from grief, from losses, from problems of every sort. Just as they are riding the crest of the wave of overcoming their condition, a kind of emotional undertow of doubt, of despair, drags them back almost to the starting point of their endeavor. It takes a stout heart to begin all over again.

I have known persons, for example, who, upon the death of a loved one, have weathered the first impact of their bereavement with great fortitude but who, weeks or even months later, when the finality of the situation strikes them, are almost powerless to stand up under the realization. Too, there are people who seem to adjust immediately to heavy financial losses, doing so with apparent control and common sense. It is only after time has shown them the real extent of their loss, in small ways as well as large ones, that they feel the undertow of despair and tend to go down in defeat, often with bitterness.

I was roused from these introspections by my friends speaking to me. The show was over. There was excited talk and laughter, and expressions of pleasure about the whole performance. One of the women in our party, taking my hands in hers, exclaimed,

"It was superb—such excitement. I am a complete wreck—limp and crumpled. And look at you—cool and fresh as when you came. Why, you don't look as if you had been to a horse show at all."

She laughed good-naturedly. She could not possibly have known how right she was.

Later, at home, Clyde said, "It was rather a dud for you, wasn't it?"

I said that I had been able to occupy my mind with one thing and another. He went on, "There is so little I can do to help you, really."

"You do a lot," I insisted.

"Oh—I can do the surface things, but no one can truly identify with another. As close as you and I are, and have been over the years, I can only guess at what goes on inside of you."

"True enough," I agreed. "No one can move into the heart of another's necessity. Actually, if that were possible, would that not be perilously close to possessiveness?"

"My position," Clyde continued, "is somewhat like that of a man in a boat accompanying a channel swimmer, and you are the swimmer. I can pass you some small sustenance, can call out words of encouragement, but it is you who must do the swimming. And it is the swimmer who knows the chill and the buffeting and the loneliness of the water."

"Very good picture," I said, "and I am certainly glad you are alongside. Will you fish me out if the water gets too rough? Right now I feel as if I might be going down for the third time."

"You'll make it," he said but I myself had my honest doubts. Thinking it over, I realized that he had put his finger on the

94

crux of the matter. I actually was in a different element now. I had moved into—rather, been thrown into—a different dimension of living. How, then, could I expect communication with other dimensions to be easy or even possible? Indeed, there were times when my inability to communicate with others in the language of my predicament drove me almost to frenzy. I was to learn that this kind of loneliness has a permanent place in my new life, as it probably has in the life of every handicapped person.

The effect of these three incidents, all occurring within a period of ten days, was oppressive. The small flame of my Self scarcely kept itself alive in this noxious air—it flickered, bent low, all but snuffed itself out.

The other problem which continually confronted me was an inexplicable fear of being left alone. True, most of us fear the strange, the unknown, and in my new condition there was an abundance of the unfamiliar. This fact, however, did not explain entirely the inordinate fear, almost terror, which seemed to bind me. This feeling had nothing to do with the loneliness of which I have just been speaking. This had to do with "aloneness" and aloneness and loneliness are not the same.

From the start of the blindness a seemingly uncontrollable fear of being left alone had manifested itself. As time went on the fear grew and grew—to such an extent, in fact, that it seemed to overshadow everything else in my life. I would become panic-stricken at the mere suggestion, even the thought, of being left alone in a room, while the idea of being left alone in the car, a restaurant or railroad station for but a few moments was too ghastly to contemplate. Under such circumstances many persons would have consulted a psychiatrist and perhaps I might have worked out of the condition with less discomfort if I myself had done so. I had the old-fashioned idea, however, that I had let myself in for this attitude and it was up to me to extricate myself from it.

I could not explain what it was that I feared in such aloneness —it was just "something." I was obsessed by the notion that I needed the presence of someone near at hand—the assurance that I was not "all by myself." Call it an *idée fixe* or whatever you like, it was a fiendish thing to live with. This was a strange manifestation and it disturbed and humiliated me, not only because of the nuisance it must have made of me to others but also because it was so foreign to my nature.

As children my brothers and I had been taught that grandfather's precept, "Do Right and Fear Not," applied to every circumstance of our life—not only to the moral aspects, like telling the truth and so forth, but also to fear of the dark, of bullies, of ghosts. The result was that we were a well-nigh fearless trio. With blindness, however, this curious, unaccountable cowardice had moved in upon me. For weeks and months, because I seldom had been left alone, the presence and power of this cowardice and its right to shadow my life had never been seriously challenged. Then one day, in a remarkable manner, the fear left me, evaporated, as it were—and I have never been afraid since. It came about in this way.

My husband had made an appointment for his periodic physical checkup and a friend had offered to stay with me during his absence. Shortly before he was due to leave the house, she was called out of town by a family emergency and we could find no one else available. This meant that, because of my silly fears, I must accompany Clyde to the doctor's office.

Suddenly, I knew I could not do it—could not, would not, embarrass him by tagging along on so personal, so private a matter as a professional visit. It was in that moment of selflessness—of thinking of another instead of myself—that I cleared the channel for good to come to me. I said to my husband,

"I think I will not go with you, after all. I won't mind staying alone for these few hours. I must start living normally sometime —why not this very hour?"

I made it sound brave and it must have carried a certain conviction for Clyde accepted my decision. It is more than likely that if he had not been so pressed for time he might have detected the bravado in my voice but, hurried as he was, he acquiesced.

I heard the starter whir, heard the car move out along the driveway, and felt that the end of the world had come. I moved slowly toward a deep-cushioned chair near the fireplace, unconsciously seeking the warmth and comfort of both. Tense, shivering, terrified to the core, I held out my hands to the burning logs. There was warmth coming from them but there was not the usual crackle and snapping of brisk burning. Even the fire was dispirited—smoldering, dully sizzling. I continued to shake, my knees and elbows fractious, out of control. How many minutes, I tried to figure, would I have to endure until I would again hear the soft swish of the tires on the driveway. He had been gone perhaps six minutes—I knew the trip would take at least two hours, one hundred and twenty minutes. How was I to occupy myself for those remaining one hundred and fourteen minutes? Moreover, I had no real assurance that my wait would be limited to two hours—it might extend itself much longer than that. My apprehension quickened.

What a boon such an afternoon would have been to me in my sighted life—I could have read, could have done some petit point, stretched strings in the garden for a new planting design. None of this was possible to me now. So what was left for me to do? Even as I formulated those words, I knew I was going to do nothing—nothing at all—for anything I might think of would take me from the safety of my chair. I knew very well that I would never move from that chair until Clyde returned. I wondered if as many as ten more minutes had passed.

As I sat there, taut and chilled, there was growing within me the conviction, the firm certainty, that soon—very soon—the vague "something" which I had been fearing for months was going to make itself manifest. During all this time I had held it at bay by keeping myself safe in the company of another person and so had never been alone and vulnerable, exposed, as I was on this afternoon. What form would this terrible dread assume—a fire, a marauder, an acute attack of some physical ailment? I could not fortell the form—all I was sure of was that this monstrous "something" would assail me at any moment now. Of course, I got what I was looking for.

Cowering there, a miserable heap of shuddering fear, I became aware of men's voices—subdued, cautious—then the scraping of shoes across the front porch, and the door chimes rang. My shaking stopped. I sat immobile, a stone woman—I did not dare answer that bell. I scarcely drew a breath. I told myself that whoever was there would go away if nobody answers. The bell rang again and through the jalousied door I heard a man's gruff voice say, "Nobody home."

Another voice, a younger, directed, "Ring again."

I dropped my head on my upturned palms. The rataplan of my heart was like the sound of a thousand tympani. I did not know what was coming—I knew only that I had now reached the end of this dead-end ditch of Stygian blackness. This moment was the nadir of my journey—the lowest measurable point.

The chime sounded again, several times and after a few seconds

I heard the sound of a key or some other metal object scratching, picking, at the lock and I guessed what was afoot. In an instant, like a lighting flash, the petrified woman I had been, metamorphosed into a flesh-and-blood woman, pulsating with indignation, with fury, that her home should be invaded.

As if in a trance I rose from my chair and turned to face the door. It was now as if I were standing apart from myself, watching myself as I walked toward the door and, astonished, hearing myself say,

"Please go away—there's a silent prayer meeting in here." My voice was low but there was unmistakable firmness in it, a kind of authority.

A second's pause—then the older man's voice burst out,

"Jesus—Joseph—and Mary!—a prayer meeting!" He spat in a revolting way.

"Let's get the hell away from here," the younger voice urged.

I heard the miserable creatures take themselves and their coarse talk away from the porch and, scuffling across the flagstones, out of my hearing.

I watched myself brush my hands together in a kind of dusting-off gesture, with a that's-that finality. I saw myself move, in a direction that was symbolic, not back to the chair, but into the center of the large living room. None of this seemed to be of my own volition—I had the eerie feeling of being a spectator.

I stood motionless—there in the middle of my house. I was distinctly conscious of an invisible shining brightness, of inaudible rich-hued music. The ham-shackles of fear were gone, and I knew with simple certainty they would never fetter me again. In that moment of freedom, in that moment of healing silence that lay all about me, in that moment of inner quietude that possessed me, I knew with crystalline clarity that I was not alone here in my darkness—that, whether I had recognized it or not, I had never been alone during any part of my journey. It was at that revealing moment that I came into a new sense—solid, real, unshakable—of the presence of God, the greatest of traveling companions.

This is the way, I suppose, that it usually happens—after the wind and the quake and the fire comes the "still, small voice." Elijah heard it that day on the mountain and I should have heard it earlier on my journey. Like most of us today, I had been too preoccupied, too busy to pick it up. Now that I was quiet, receptive, a kind of peace, cool and soothing, enveloped me. I began to wonder—was the prayer, earnest and sincere, which I had made so many months before, being answered—the prayer that the blindness be blessed. The unreasoning fear of being left alone was already gone—would not the other burdnes which blindness had brought be, in their turn, lifted too—the doubts, the disappointments, even the terrible loneliness?

Almost at once I had an answer about the last named, for there rose up in my recollection some lines which Bernard Shaw wrote for his great play, *St. Joan*—lines which might have been written, I felt, for me and this moment:

"I see now that the loneliness of God is His strength. Well, my loneliness shall be my strength too. It is better to be alone with God—His friendship will not fail me, nor His counsel, nor His love. In His strength I will dare, and dare, and dare until I die."

Thus it was that, although I had lost my way for a little while, I was back on the right path now and eager to continue my journey. I stooped and began to collect the scattered luggage of my spirit. I adjusted the weight of the Black Beast and, cradling the reviving flame of my Self against any sudden gust, I set out afresh—across the last stretches of the Dark Place, toward its outer rim which was the border, the frontier, of a better land.

Curiously enough, the music that sang within me as I plodded along was not some majestic strain from a great oratorio, an opera, or a symphony. Instead, it was that haunting bit from the Broadway musical, *Carousel:*

> When you walk through a storm
> Keep your head up high
> And don't be afraid of the dark—

That is the way it begins and it ends with the words and the music familiar to many audiences:

> AND YOU'LL NEVER WALK ALONE

I had found myself a marching song.

CHAPTER 7

I Cross the Frontier

SOMEONE—I cannot learn who it was—once wrote that "the rim of shadow is the line of light." I found it just that simple—for, at the instant that I crossed the rim of shadow, I also crossed the line of light. They are one and the same. It is what lies on either side of this subtle boundary that counts, that makes the difference.

When I moved across that boundary, that frontier line, I ceased being an emigrant from the Dark Place, a despondent, troubled creature fleeing its hold. Instead, I became, with that crossing, an immigrant, sensible of the difference and especially of the fact that somewhere ahead there was light, illumination, for my spirit.

One difference at this point was that my attitude was reversing itself—instead of propelling myself away from something, much like a runner or swimmer trying to put distance behind him, I now surrendered myself to the pull of something ahead. I had ceased to throw the weight of desire and effort into escaping the dark—rather, my hope and effort now turned toward the illumination whose force I was beginning to feel.

As an immigrant I had, in the way of immigrants down through the ages, a deep yearning to identify with the new country. I had the ardent desire to possess this new land and in turn to be possessed by it. It seemed to invite me to activity and there grew within me the lively and eager determination to explore this domain, not only for myself but for others who might be more timid, less venturesome than I.

Although the greatest illumination seemed to lie ahead, there was, from the moment I entered this new territory, light all about me. Faint at first, it daily grew stronger and steadier.

One day that light threw a searching beam full upon something which astonished me—it revealed to me that I had never actually accepted the fact of blindness. I had realized it, yes—but realization and acceptance, I suddenly saw, are not the same thing at all. That I had not accepted the blindness had been subtly hidden from my conscious thinking and two errors had grown out of this situation.

In the first place, I must have been regarding the blindness as a temporary state—been maintaing to myself that this was an ephemeral, fleeting condition. Somewhere beneath the surface I must have been telling myself that I was just marking time—was masquerading all the while and some day the mask would come off and I would see again, and all this foolish, difficult, adjusting kind of living arrangement would be tossed aside and I could forget the whole tedious business.

103

The second error I had been guilty of was that, although I had learned to do many things in this hampered, constricting kind of existence, I had been operating almost entirely with a sighted person's approach. I had not been making a proper allowance—a proper "tret," if you will, for the blind factor. Both of these errors were evasions, and whether we discern it or not, any form of evasion—hypocrisy, pretense, deception, insincerity—tends to wear one down, emotionally, mentally, physically. As Anne Morrow Lindbergh wrote in her *Gift from the Sea:*

"The most exhausting thing in life, I have discovered, is being insincere."

I had been guilty of the worst kind of insincerity—self-deception.

When I was very new-blind, I could not bring myself to admit the blindness. I would endeavor to explain my fumblings with such phrases as, "I have some difficulty in seeing" or "My eyesight is rather poor," and so forth. I shrank from using the word "blind"—it was so blunt, so brutal, so final. As time went on, I saw the need for admitting my handicap but even then I did so only on the surface—underneath, my sighted mind was directing all my efforts with a "business as usual" attitude. When, however, the clear light of the new land revealed my nonacceptance, I faced myself:

"Now look—how long are you going to keep up this cowardly flim-flam. You know you are blind and you know, too, that, short of some new technic or some old, old miracle, you are going to be blind to the end of your life. There is nothing temporary about this. Why not toss all that subterfuge out the window and admit you have limits, and learn to respect them."

Conversations between me and myself rarely last long—and

the outcome of this brief one was that I relinquished, abandoned, the evasiveness I had been hugging to my heart.

It was astonishing to note how difficulties now seemed to burn off, much as a fog burns off under a strong sun. I now addressed my activities with great lightness of spirit, with an invincible kind of buoyancy I had not known in a long time. Being absolved of the burden of nonacceptance, I was freed of its accompanying tension. I was reminded of the words Chaucer gives to Cressida in that ancient tale. Whatever else Cressida was—and, reportedly, she was several things—she was a woman who insisted on being herself. As Chaucer set it down:

"I, Criseyde, am myne owene womman, wel at ese."

I myself, by the grace of God, was again my own woman, and well at ease.

True "acceptance" does not mean an attitude of negative resignation, a sorrowful mien, a wringing of the hands in self-pity, thereby distressing those about one. Rather, "acceptance," as I understand and use the term, means to look squarely at a troublesome situation, then to proceed from there to do whatever is possible within the framework of that situation. It is much like accepting a hand dealt in a card game—there it is, make the most you can out of it. To outplay one's opponents at bridge is an exciting pastime but to accept the challenge of seemingly impossible conditions in one's life and outface them, is far more exciting, far more substantial, more rewarding.

As I thought about these things, there was borne in upon me the plight of many persons suffering, in one way or another, from their nonacceptance of the framework of their existence. There are families, for instance, who seem never to have learned that money is not elastic—who do not accept the cold fact that their income is not sufficient to cover the kind of life they endeavor to lead. This situation generates an almost unbearable tension for these unhappy, muddled people so that they do not enjoy what they do have, and often this is more than modest.

There are parents who seem unable, or unwilling, to accept the fact that they have not the right to try to live their lives all over again in the lives of their children—children who perhaps have neither the desire nor the capacity to follow the life pattern which their parents have drawn for them.

If we would only be honest—with ourselves especially—and say, This is the way things are, and start from there, we could, without the burdensome excess baggage of nonacceptance, go so much farther—and go faster.

For me one of the most difficult forms of acceptance was the accepting of help from others. I had always been a self-sufficient person, a kind of freestanding spirit, and in my new kind of life I often rebelled at being tethered by blindness. No longer could I get into my car and dash off to attend speedily to some errand, or pick up a friend and go on to some social affair. Now I had to wait to be taken, by family or friend. No longer could I go—unattended and unassisted—to choose clothes, draperies, gifts and all the rest of shopping. I accepted this necessary assistance—I was obliged to. To be sure, this developed within me a certain patience, but up to then patience, alas, was a commodity in which I had seldom dabbled.

The art of acceptance is a very real thing, not just a well-turned phrase. To advance in this art requires both study and practice. One soon learns that there is a great difference in the manner in which assistance is given. Some persons help so quietly, so deftly, that the deficiency of a handicapped individual goes almost unnoticed. There are others, however, who make a real "production" out of the simplest assistance, thereby causing the recipient to feel very conspicuous, very apologetic.

I can never forget my distress at a ladies' luncheon when the fellow-guest at my right "managed" everything for me. Her desire to help me was touching but I became utterly fatigued with trying to dodge the unpredictable, unannounced movements of her hands about my plate as she reached across to get my soup spoon and put it into the soup, "all nice and ready for you," and later to get the fork and arrange it "real handy" on my plate. Since I was accustomed to doing all these things for myself, I grew more and more confused. The final torment came with the dessert, which was sliced fresh peaches. Over my protest as well as over the peaches, she poured a lavish amount of cream and then, scooping up a spoonful at a time, she passed the spoon to me, adominishing me to "Chew it well." At the end I fully expected her to say, "Now, let me wipe your little mouth and take off your bib."

This was one woman's idea of help—at the other extreme is the blessed person who says in a low voice, "Let me know if you want help with anything."

Gradually I became reconciled to accepting favors from others —in fact I came to see clearly that without acceptance on some-body's part, there could be no giving. And what would this world be without the joy of giving?

After I had ceased to shrink from the admission that I was blind, I went even farther and openly volunteered the informa-tion. I did this by carrying—with no diffidence at all—a white cane. To the blind, a white cane is—to filch a phrase from Shylock—"the badge of all our tribe." Many children refer to me as "the lady with the white cane." I love this descriptive title—it somehow manages to convey how inseparable the little cane and I are. My cane was a good friend's present to me and thus is a double delight for, previous to my first feel of this one, I had known only very masculine editions of canes—heavy crookneck affairs. There was, too, the retractable metal type that telescopes into what is called the baton. When extended, this kind is so long that it seemed like a shepherd's crook in my hand, making me feel part of a Millet canvas or, more fanciful still, one of those beplumed Empire ladies who affected long staffs. Whatever else it might have been, it was of no practical help to me.

Then one happy day the perfect cane entered my life. It is of bamboo, light weight, feminine, and easy to manage. Painted white, it has, looped at the base of its small head, a silk cord. I have these cords in several colors—navy, brown, beige (and a bright red one for Christmas)—so that I can always match the basic color of my dress. The cane is sturdy but so light that, as it hangs from my wrist, it has little more weight than the average bracelet. I never use it at home because I know intimately every inch of our house, but whenever I leave our premises, the cane is swinging from my wrist. It is my custom, when walking along the street or moving about in crowds, to slip my left hand through the arm of the person I am walking with, thus giving my right hand and arm freedom to "operate" the cane.

I am always somewhat amused at reports about satellites in outer space sending back code signals to the earth to be interpreted here. My little cane does better than that—it does not stop with codes, it transmits openly. All the while I am walking about, perhaps at the same time engaging in a lively conversation, the little cane is sending me information about my surroundings and I am picking it up. "Be wary of these steps—they are shallow and pitch a bit; this carpet is laid over a very thick lining; watch for the step-off when you come to the edge; the furniture here is arranged in tight little groupings which is comforting, but there are rugs all over the place. Watch out for them." And so it goes—whether I am crossing highly polished surfaces, pebbly walks or grassy stretches—whether I am gauging the height of a curb or orienting myself in unfamiliar quarters, this "eye-upon-the-ground" never fails me. To be sure, the cane gets considerably scuffed up with all such nosings-about but a new coat of paint quickly restores its pristine freshness.

In the beginning of our partnership, the cane and I did not realize how very "snoopy" we were. There was always the strong temptation to explore everything in our immediate vicinity until one day, while visiting in a friend's house, she said, very quietly,

"My dear, you do not realize it but your cane is coming perilously close to my jade."

She has some rare pieces which she keeps on a fine old etagere. I was appalled, but how I loved her for telling me in just that fashion. She could so easily have said that she thought I would "be happier in some other chair." This woman of exquisite manners, however, gently put the matter up to me. From that time on, I knew that the place for my cane when I go visiting is the safe and quiet space beneath my chair.

Whenever I stay overnight in a strange bedroom, my cane and I explore the location of each piece of furniture the moment I come into the room. This provides me with a clear picture of where the various "obstacles" are—obstacles that usually are hazards as well. Not long ago I visited old friends at their plantation home. I had often been their guest, but the bedroom I was given on this visit was one I had never occupied before. Arriving about cocktail time I stayed downstairs until time to dress for dinner. When I reached my room, my things had been un-packed and the maid was just bringing back my dinner dress which she had pressed. At once I went about the room with my cane, noting the exact location of the dresser, the bed, the several chairs and the bathroom fixtures. I felt comfortably certain then about everything and the maid left.

I was well along with my dressing when, in passing near the bed—crack—something struck me between the eyes, struck hard. The blow seemed to come from nowhere—an awful blow on my forehead. I drew back, puzzled, then felt my way along the foot of the bed to what I thought might be safer territory when —bang—I was struck again. I began to wonder if this old house might be infested with a poltergeist, for I was certain—absolutely certain—that there was nothing but the bed in this part of the room.

"See here," I protested aloud to whoever or whatever was responsible for the surprise attack, "this is not at all funny."

I had come to the corner of the bed and something impelled me to explore the corner piece. My fingers followed it up and up—it was carved. I traced the carving and at the top was a large pineapple finial. No one had thought to mention to me that this was a fourposter bed—and the cane and I had explored only at mattress height. As a result, I had been assaulted by a pineapple, traditional symbol of hospitality. I was not really hurt and the encounter made a good story at the dinner table but, for as long as I occupied that room, I scouted those bedposts by waving my arms before me as I approached the bed. I reminded myself of the Rhine maidens in *The Ring* who perpetually weave their arms about as they swim here and there. I thoroughly enjoyed the rest of my visit, but must admit that I was glad to leave off being a Rhine maiden.

The cane and I get along marvelously until someone seizes upon the idea of "helping" us. I have boundless gratitude for such an outgoing impulse and I am most appreciative of true helpfulness. All too often, however, I have come dangerously close to a bad tumble because someone had an ill-conceived urge to help. Just as I near a flight of steps or the curb at a street crossing and am attentive to what the cane is telling me, some misguided person will grasp the elbow of my "cane-arm" and lift it so that the tip of the cane, my one and only "eye-upon-the-world" is rendered wholly useless. Even when I explain that I must have the cane-arm free in order to insure my safety, such persons invariably reply,

"But that is exactly what I am doing—keeping you safe."

Sometimes my blood runs cold when such an "attack" of help comes suddenly. I love these people for the warmth of their intent but I often wish their heads might work as fast as their hearts.

In so many ways the cane grew to be an important part of my life, a trusted instrument of communication in this new land. There was another channel of communication, however, which I began to long for—the old habit of letter writing was begging to be reestablished.

I had always engaged in a rather wide personal correspondence. My friends continued to write me warm letters of friendliness and encouragement which I loved receiving, and I so wished to reply to them with something more than a message sent through someone else. I could not expect my husband to write letters of this kind for me—I knew I must devise some way to do it myself. It was natural that I thought only of handwriting for that was the only kind I had ever employed. My first attempts at writing produced lines that wandered and "strayed like lost

111

sheep" across and up and down the pasture of the page. Nobody, I was told, could read it. I realized I must have something to guide me along a straight line. Using a large size tablet, I laid across it a foot ruler and held it in place with rubber bands. Writing a line at a time, I would move the ruler down the page after each line. The spaces were uneven and the lines were not always parallel but communicate I must, and I began to answer the stack of letters. If I had needed proof of my friends' devotion, this provided it for my writing must have presented a maddening puzzle with its deformed, anemic, stunted characters, hippety-hopping over the page. My friends were not only faithful, they were also patient for they deciphered those scrawls, those hiero-glyphics. They must have, for I began to receive replies, and not in vague terms but in direct response to what I had written.

Shortly afterward we found, at the Lighthouse in New York, the ridged board used by many blind writers. This is a corrugated sheet of cardboard over which the letter paper is laid and both clamped to a board of the same size. The writing is done between the ridges and the feeling of accuracy and solidity was a welcome one. My inclination was to write in letters that were rather too large and I was constantly under stress of reducing their size, but this method was vastly superior to the ruler and elastic bands, although I am sure that my writing, at times continued to be difficult to read.

Frequently I thought of how convenient it would be if I only knew how to use a typewriter—but a typewriter's keyboard had always seemed more formidable than a piano's. The idea grew that here was something for me to try. A blind person should be a "natural" for the Touch System. I discovered, early in 1956, that among the recordings of the Talking Books there was a course

112

in typing—precisely the same as one would pursue in a regular school. I asked that a set of these records be sent to me and the day they arrived was as exciting as Matriculation Day at college. Here was real adventure.

As I listened to the opening paragraphs of the lessons, spoken by one of their best readers, I knew additional gratitude for the Talking Book, for here, concisely but with understanding, and step by step, was everything that could be taught to the beginner. I am willing to admit that my initial enthusiasm sometimes flagged as the days went by and the tricky business of pinpointing the instruction tended to fatigue me. I kept telling myself, however, that all this novitiate drudgery would be forgotten in the joy of writing my first letter on this clattering contrivance.

Hour after hour I followed the voice as it intoned the spelling of words—pronouncing the syllables slowly at first, then stepping up the tempo with each repetition until the final one was done at a really brisk pace.

At first it was baffling to spell out consciously every word as I put it down. I think much handwriting is almost automatic as regards spelling but in the early months of typing I actually "spelled out"—letter by letter—every word. This was necessary because I had no way to check by eye—I had to be sure in my mind. Somewhat later I suddenly found myself putting down each word as a whole with never a thought of its component letters, nor even of the communicating machinery of arms, hands, and fingers. Unquestionably, what is sometimes referred to as finger articulation or as digital dexterity developed through years at the piano keyboard accelerated my progress. My main problem was to transpose this ability to another medium.

The sense of freedom I experienced on the day I wrote my

113

first letter, directed the envelope, sealed and stamped it is something I cannot adequately put into words. I had now pulled abreast of my fellows. Today, aside from having incoming mail read to me, I take care of all our correspondence and I never regard it as heavy or tiring—indeed, it is one of my chief pleasures. An additional satisfaction came when, later on, I achieved my goal of typing my own manuscripts.

My typing problems, naturally enough, vary from those of a sighted person—sometimes to my advantage, sometimes to my disadvantage. For example, I am spared that moment of confusion when one looks at the word just written and wonders if that is actually the correct spelling. I am sure that everyone who can write has had this puzzling experience. The spelling seems right enough as you set it down but the longer you look at it, the more doubtful you become until, in the end, you reach for the dictionary to settle the matter. With me this never happens—a word goes down on the paper just as it flashes through my mind and there it is—fixed, accomplished, trusted. This slight edge of benefit, however, is offset by tedious drawbacks. For instance as I, a blind woman, write, I must rivet my attention firmly not only on what is now going down on the paper and which, of course, I do not see, but also on what the line just above consisted of. It is more than a litttle irksome not to be able to snatch at so immediate a past and use it as a springboard, a gangplank, for what is immediately ahead. The present instant —or the instant present if you prefer—is the only hard, sure reality. I miss the ability to move freely across the page with the eye, and often feel mutinous at this rigid immobility. But of what avail?

One devastating experience I have, and not infrequently, is that I become so engrossed in what I am writing I do not notice when

I come to the bottom of the page but continue to write on, line after line. Suddenly I become conscious of the difference in the sound of the machine and, reaching up to investigate, find that the paper has long since shot out from the roller. Then I must go back and reconstruct as best I can what I had written only on the roller. It is usually a difficult business to recall it, word for word, and invariably I have the conviction that what was lost was the best work I had done in days.

During the tedious weeks and months of training myself in this new way of living, I was acutely aware of the fact that it was a very protected, a very routine, way, and I sometimes wondered what I might do if in some emergency I might have to act on my own initiative. Did I still possess, as I had heretofore possessed, the ability to make a split-second response to the unexpected? How would I behave under stress or need for sudden decision? One spring day an incident occurred that served to reassure me.

My husband, like most American men, is a lover of sports. One sport is closer to his heart than all the rest—track and field competition. This interest dates back to his college days when he himself competed in such events. He has never missed a track meet that he could possibly attend—the indoor meets at Madison Square Garden, the Penn relays, the Olympic tryouts, and others less widely known. Recently the university in our town was host to the South East Conference meet and for weeks Clyde had been looking forward to this occasion.

During the morning of the day of the meet he assembled the assorted paraphernalia he always takes with him—things to enhance his pleasure and comfort. There was his special visored cap, his stop watch, dark glasses, pencils and erasers, binoculars to be slung about his neck, a thick foam rubber cushion. He had an early luncheon so as to arrive at the stadium in ample time to secure a good parking spot as well as a desirable seat high in the stand. Reserved seats for this event are sold by section rather than by individual seat. Thus to arrive early insures getting a cool comfortable seat in the shadow of the press box instead of sitting under the direct rays of the sun for four long oven-hot hours.

It is my custom to ask him, when he is dressed to go out, what he is wearing. I have a great interest in his appearance and the factor of blindness has not produced indifference on my part. Replying to my usual question he said, "A long-sleeved blue plaid cotton shirt, light blue slacks, my special cap, buckskin loafers."

"Sounds nice and cool," I said. "By the way, what time is it?"

"Oh, lord," he exclaimed, looking at his watch, "I'm afraid I'm going to be late after all."

Hurriedly he snatched up the items he had placed on a table near the door and dashed out to the car. "Now I've really got to hurry. 'Bye." And he was gone.

I tidied up the luncheon things and then, in making sure that the outer door was latched, my fingers touched what seemed to be a leather strap over the doorknob. I investigated. It was a leather strap, and it was attached to the binoculars.

"Oh, no," I cried out in protest to the empty house. "Don't tell me he has forgotten his field glasses." I stood rooted to the spot. This was disaster for a track meet without glasses would be only half a track meet to Clyde. Perhaps, I thought, he will miss them before he gets very far and will come back for them. Inasmuch as some time had elapsed since he left, however, I doubted if this would happen.

116

A burning indignation ran through me—not only that he should miss the full enjoyment of the afternoon but that this horrid blindness barred me from what I would already be doing if I had sight—taking them to him.

"But now," I groaned, "I am pinioned in this house."

Then, something inside me asked, "Are you?"

I hesitated. Was it possible that I need not be pinioned in this house—need the fact that never in my blindness had I ventured out alone matter to me now? Here was my chance to do something for one who had done so much for me.

I moved toward the telephone, dialed my trusted Information. I could not recall the name of any taxicab company, since we seldom had occasion to call a cab. Information read me the few companies listed and I chose the one that sounded speedy. I was overjoyed when the taxi office assured me they would have a cab at my house in less than ten minutes. While I waited I gathered up my white cane, swung the binoculars about my neck and put several silver dollars in my pocket. Silver coins are the only kind of money I feel safe about counting.

When the cab drew up in front of our house I was waiting at the front door, my white cane plainly visible as information that I needed help. The driver, however, did not "get the message." He merely tapped his horn. But when he saw me start groping along with my cane, he left the car and hastened to me.

"Oh, lady, I did not know—" he began.

"That's all right," I told him as I climbed in. "I am blind, and I need your help. I want you to drive me as fast as you can—legally—to the track meet at the stadium."

I heard him gasp and he made no move to start. I could guess what was running through his mind—Can I risk carrying such a passenger? For unquestionably she must be crazy—a blind

117

woman with binoculars, going to a track meet, and in a hurry.

"Come on, fellow," I urged him. "I know what I am doing."

On the way to the stadium I told him my problem—that I must get these glasses to my husband who had forgotten them. "I want you to drive to the entrance nearest the press box and then, while I wait in the cab, I want you to take the glasses to my husband. He will probably be in one of the shady seats under the press box." I then described Clyde and how he was dressed. Then the thought came to me that Clyde might become anxious if he knew I had come out alone on such a sortie and would possibly leave the meet to drive me home, so I added, "It is not necessary to tell my husband that I came along—just tell him that I sent the glasses as a surprise."

Sitting alone in the the taxi gave me the chance to savor my adventure. I could hear the cheers of the crowd inside the stadium, the sharp crack of the starter's gun, the great groan when somebody must have missed—maybe dropped a baton in a relay. To me that was the ultimate calamity. There was a fresh spring breeze wandering about but the sun beat mercilessly on the roof of the cab. For a woman who was trying in every possible way to lead a near-normal life, this was exciting, rewarding. I had dared something and it was working out. To the sighted this would undoubtedly seem a trivial experience but to me it was another step on my journey. The taste of even this much self-sufficiency was sweet on my tongue—so sweet in fact that I hoped the driver would take a long time to deliver those binoculars. I wished I had told him to take time to watch one race.

When he returned, the driver reported he had no trouble in locating my husband. "I spotted that plaid shirt even up there in the shade. The gentleman was sure glad to get his field glasses."

"You remembered to say nothing about my being out here?"
I asked.

"I remembered—like you said that might have worried him,
you out here in this heat. He's having himself a lot of fun." Then
as he swung the car around he said as a kind of afterthought to
himself, "I didn't know so many girls go to track meets."

I laughed heartily. That's fine, too, I said to myself. He is having his fun and I'm having mine.

Arrived at home I asked the driver what the meter registered.
"Half a dollar—just the fare from the stadium, ma'am. Your husband paid me for the fare down and a good tip besides. Helping
me from the cab, he chuckled, "You know, this wasn't a bad
trip, after all."

After all—bless him—he had taken me as a passenger although
at the start he was convinced that I was a lunatic. Furthermore,
he—although he did not know it—had helped me to negotiate,
on my own, my first outside excursion.

In fact, everyone I met helped me in one way or another, and
I was grateful. These kindnesses toward me might occur at any
time, in any place. It was at parties, however, that thoughtfulness
was manifested in abundance. I had always loved parties—large
parties, small parties, luncheon, dinner, or afternoon parties—but
just enough of them to provide high spots in my life. A constant
routine of parties can become as monotonous as a constant routine of work. Either extreme can be a bore. Occasional parties
add zest as well as relaxation to life.

I must confess that, when I first began going to parties after
becoming blind, I experienced a nervous kind of constraint. I
knew this was due to the fact that Clyde and I were strangers
among people who knew each other well and also because I had

the added difficulty of being unable to recognize people by sight. Recognition by ear came later. At that time it was at parties, too, that the loneliness of isolation attacked me and I had to fight mightily to conquer it. After I had come into the consciousness of the Presence and knew I could draw courage and strength at any time from the Great Reservoir, I noted that a certain relaxed attitude began to develop. This being true, in no time at all others responded to it and soon I came to the stage where I really forgot that I was different.

It was then that parties again became fun for me. In addition to the sheer pleasure of being with those I like, parties offer me an opportunity to study people, to get to know them. I find renewal in the witty stories, the quick badinage, the general air of liveliness. Once in a while, oddly enough, I get hurt at parties but I learn something from that, too.

Handicapped persons must develop a kind of shatterproof defense against unexpected, painful, reminders of their handicap. Such defense can never render them completely invulnerable. I myself am usually on guard against such desolating experiences but now and again something unlooked-for strikes. My discomfiture may not be apparent to those about me but inwardly I am completely routed.

Something of this sort happened to me at a party recently and what was especially devastating about the occurrence was that I myself was responsible for the turn of the conversation. It was a gay and beautiful party and among other decorations there were bowls of violets on several tables. As I breathed in their incomparable fragrance I was whisked back to my childhood when we always had loads of these lovely flowers. Impulsively I said to the group about me,

"Oh, I wonder if little King Solomon is still bathing his feet."

"What on earth are you talking about?" one friend asked, puzzled.

"I'll show you," I said, and feeling my way among the violets, I drew out one and stripped off its petals. This was wholly automatic as I had done it so often as a child. Then I held up what was left, saying,

"There he is—King Solomon himself—look!"

At their expressions of delight at what they saw, I myself was seized with a natural impulse to have a look and, in that brief moment, the flash of time it took me to turn my hand so that I might glimpse the miniature royalty, I forgot that I was blind. Caught up in a remembered excitement from childhood, I wanted, with an almost uncontrollable yearning, to see this foolish whimsy imagined in the cup of a violet—tiny King Solomon sitting so straight and proud, a gold crown on his head, his skinny little legs in a tub.

The expectation collapsed—I was, of course, looking at nothing, even less than nothing for disappointment always carries a negative sign. I froze. Oddly enough, no one in the group had ever known this trick and everyone was so beguiled by it, so engrossed in passing the little fellow from hand to hand, that no one noticed my discomfort, my real pain which was running hot and deep.

"You know more amusing things, Marie," said one of the group.

And a good thing it is, I said to myself but I vowed I would never again risk torture by looking for the king who lives in a violet. It was the unexpected factor in this incident that intensified my hurt.

121

This factor of the unexpected brought me, at another time, a very different reaction, a very pleasurable one. Someone had sent me a large bouquet of mignonette—the large-trussed kind. I adore the fragrance of mignonette—it is as delicate as humility, as haunting as the recollection of first love. I set the vase of flowers on my dresser and luxuriated in their subtle perfume as I dressed for the evening. So powerful is the association between the senses and the emotions that suddenly I seemed to be dressing for a party in my late teens. The appointments on the dresser, as I touched them, seemed the same, as did even the dress, and the string of pearls. It was arresting, this association. I stood still, perfectly quiet—and at once I was eighteen again. Then I did what no sighted woman of mature years would dare to do—dare to look into her mirror with the excited, confident expectation of seeing her own youth reflected there. My sightless eyes saw not what I must look like today, but what I wanted to see there—a girl with fresh young skin, clear blue eyes and red-blonde hair.

I had a wonderful time gazing at myself as I used to be. Who could contradict me about what I was seeing—myself least of all. It is rare that I indulge in such fancy but the experience was more than pleasant—it was downright heady.

While at a party one evening I suddenly remembered that I had forgoten to phone an important message to a committee chairman. I asked my hostess if I might use her telephone.

"But of course," she said. "Come, I'll take you. The phone in the study will be best."

When we reached the study doorway she said,

"Just a moment—I will turn on the light. It is pitch-dark in there."

"Please don't trouble," I begged. "It will make no difference to me, you know," but I heard the click of the switch and she guided me to the desk and chair, placed my hand on the telephone.

"I'll come back for you—say, in about ten minutes?" She left.

I dialed the number and received the busy signal. While waiting to dial again I thought of my hostess's remark about giving me some light. She had not done so, of course. With the best will in the world, she could not do so. To her, the room was now lighted—to me it was still dark. I fell to thinking of how mine is a portable kind of darkness—I carry it with me wherever I go.

I froze with horror as the full import of these words struck me. What a wretched, wretched thought. Had I, in some way, been guilty of projecting my physical darkness into all my surroundings—into the lives of the people about me? There in that quiet study, with laughter from the party coming faintly from another part of the house, I hastily reviewed the situation and determined that I would set about replacing anything like portable darkness with portable light. Because of the blindness I might resemble a dark lantern but, inside the dark lantern, the small flame would burn steady, bright.

I finally got my call through and was just finishing the conversation when my hostess returned for me. As we left the room I asked,

"Don't you want to turn off the light?"

As she snapped the switch she said, half musingly, "I wonder—when I turn off the light, do I turn on the darkness?"

"Perhaps," I said, "but the important thing is that for me you turned on the light." There was a double meaning here that she could not have guessed.

On a recent visit out of town Clyde and I were guests at a beautiful dinner. The man on my right seemed rather younger than the rest of us, judging from his voice and manner. When I asked—merely to start the conversation—his opinion on a certain subject, he gave it to me—the whole of it—and with gusto. I liked him and I liked the way he viewed himself as well as the rest of his world. When I asked him his field of activity—in other words, how he made a living—he replied very briskly,

"I am a specialist in generalization."

This struck me as rather novel and I asked for more. He obliged, tossing about such bewildering phrases as "immaterial actuality," "the complexities of the simple" (or was it "the simplicity of the complex").

I limped along as best I could, but when he referred to "the height of the Depression" I balked. I had lived through that Depression and there was no height at all, only depth, sickening, abysmal depth. He agreed that this might very well have been the case but, he wanted to know, did I never use such contradictory phrases for emphasis? They were, he insisted, great fun to originate. I made no comment for the only contradiction I could think of at that moment was that *Waltzing Matilda* is a March. Of course I could not have offered so frivolous a reply to so serious a young man. Serious he certainly was and an extremely keen observer.

Coffee was served on the large glassed-in veranda and my young man brought my demitasse to me. He inquired if he might give me some sugar and there was such pleading in his voice that I accepted, although I loathe sugar in coffee.

"At last I can do something for you," he said and sat down beside me. "All during dinner I watched for an opportunity to be of some service to you but you were so competent about everything—the soup, the roast, the wine glass. I was certain you would need help when the dessert plate was brought but—no—

you picked up the doily and finger bowl and deposited them as deftly as anybody else at the table."

I am as "mune" to a compliment—direct or implied—as the next woman, and this praise was like a bright red cherry topping an already pleasant evening.

He chuckled as he continued. "And now, at last, you let me give you a lump of sugar."

"That makes me feel rather like a horse," I said, and we both burst into laughter.

He was not finished, however, for he suddenly cried out, almost as if in pain.

"—but this blindness must be such a damned inconvenience!"

I caught my breath, set my small cup on the low table. This chap, with his keen and trained mind, had cut cleanly to the marrow, to the pith of the nature of blindness. No one else—not even myself—had ever expressed it so succinctly, so ultimately, for, every hour of every day, blindness is meshed with inconvenience, is permeated with it, soaked in it. I sometimes feel that the very air I breathe is loaded with inconvenience.

I still have an affection for that nice young man and I am sorry that his work has taken him far from our orbit. He gave me so much to carry away with me that evening, not the least of which was a healthy brusqueness in dealing with problems.

Inconvenience is not limited to the blind, however. Every handicapped person must contend with its vexations. I had this brought home to me on another evening, at another party. I was sitting alone on a small sofa when our hostess brought over a man whom she introduced as, "someone you will find very congenial." She moved on and at once the man confided,

"I am very deaf but I have been studying lip reading, and al-

125

though I may ask you to repeat an occasional phrase, I believe I can follow most of your conversation."

How considerate it was of him to volunteer this information at once. My white cane had probably established for him the fact that I could not see. So—there we were—thrown together, to make what we could of the situation. As a matter of fact, we did rather well—this charming man with a delicately crisp sense of humor, engaging me in a conversation that covered much more than mere small talk. To anybody who had taken the trouble to observe us, we must have presented a fantastic sight as we sat there—a deaf man trying to hear with his eyes, a blind woman trying to see with her ears.

Was there something of synesthesia here?

A thoughtful flavor was added to a small gathering of very congenial persons one late winter afternoon. In the group was a man well-loved by all of us. He is a person of great charm, of gentle manners. He is the kind every hostess leans on—not the jovial, life-of-the-party sort, but an amiable and witty individual who can nudge others into being their best. Over the years he has—to use a man's expression—"learned to roll with the punches." His humor is usually of the sparkling variety but on this afternoon he seemed somewhat preoccupied, thoughtful rather than gay. We learned later that he had just come from a hospital where a close friend was very ill.

During a lull in the conversation, and apropos of nothing at all, he said, very quietly,

"I often think that life is much like a train—and all of us are aboard. One by one, as our stop is called, we get off this train."

It was a simple statement, with no gloomy intonation. All who heard it seemed receptive of it but not in the least depressed by it. General conversation picked up again, but for a while I sat silent for the remark had shown me that mine was a singular situation.

Like the others, I was on board that train—but the Beast and I were riding on one ticket. I fell to wondering if, when my stop is called and I leave the train, will the Beast get off with me?

CHAPTER 8

Traveler's Rest

BEFORE today's palatial motels, with their proud baronial names, lined the highways of our nation, the motorist's best chance for comfortable overnight accommodations was to be found in some fine old country home that had been converted into a Guest House. Usually such places bore simple names— Twin Pines, Shady Lawn, Mountain View—but the one that invariably drew me was Traveler's Rest. There seemed to be one place of this name on every road and generally it gave what it promised—rest. Here one could put a stop to the day's mileage, relax and refresh one's self. Such a place was a kind of plateau from which one could review today's trip and plan for tomorrow's.

In my journey from the Dark Place I had now reached some

such point—a plateau of endeavor where I could pause for a while, ease up a bit, take a Traveler's Rest. Here was my opportunity—and I felt strongly the importance of doing this—to reevaluate everything in my life. Here was the spot where I could, as the wireless operators term it, get a "fix" on my present position.

It was like drawing up a great balance sheet—this reviewing of my position—noting and weighing the gains against the losses. Heading the long list of my losses is the one word, LIGHT. It is light that infuses into human life a quality which animates everything we do. Light is the drama of existence. Light brings delineation to the formless, and ignites a blaze of color across the drab. Used as some photographers use it, light is substance.

The one word "light," however, can scarcely convey either the extent or the details of my deprivation. When light, the keystone, was taken away, the whole arch of my life was loosened, so that it fell apart. What had always been a substantial structure now lay about me in scattered desolation.

I often think of this pure bounty of light as the great taproot from which springs the long list of other losses. Directly stemming from this basic loss of light is a trio—the loss of color, of form, of movement.

Color is almost a life-giving property in the life of most persons—great splashes of it or small bits. I keenly miss it from my life—the whole wide range of it, the full chromatic scale of its gradations. Today I must continually needle my memory to renew the recollection of color, for it is a fugitive thing, draining itself quickly from the memory.

Form, too, is a part of everyday life from which I am separated. I yearn for its many aspects and dimensions—design, symmetry, asymmetry. I miss the sudden thrust of a skyscraper, the varying

129

forms of human hands, young and old, the intricate patterns of flowers. The small clove-pink, for instance, whose redolent perfume I can still enjoy, can no longer charm me with its form—those tiny petals so deftly gathered in, their serrated edges looking as if the Great Designer had cut about their rims with diminutive pinking shears to give them added interest.

Gone from my life, too, is movement, for today my receptivity in that regard is at the dead-still. Gone are those beautiful arcs and lines of movement that delight the eye and lift the heart—the darting of a hummingbird, the rhythmic play of a great fountain, the graceful skimming of young men over a flight of hurdles.

True, I can summon recollections of many of these things, some of them are quite sharp, but at best, such recollections are what might be termed reproductions, not the originals, and I am never unaware of the difference.

Closely related to this trio of things that I miss is something that I can best describe by the term of "The Look of Today"—the look of my contemporary world. I miss this—miss it terribly—the look of what is going on all about me, every day—what, in short, I am missing because my sight is missing. To be sure, through the radio, the Talking Books, and what is read to me from other material, I can keep abreast of world happenings, and of current report and comment on politics, the arts, science. I can, however, go just so far through these media and there I must stop. There is still so much beyond this point that I miss—so much that only my own two eyes could show me. What, I often ask myself, must all this look like—this panorama of today?

No matter how good and understanding my friends' intentions may be, they can not tell me precisely what I myself might see in a landscape, a photograph, a frock. Something which my background and past experience would make important to me may escape them quite completely, for they are catching what their tastes, their interests, impel them to see. It is natural that we tend to screen out what is of lesser interest to ourselves. I accept this fact and I accept the further fact that all descriptions I receive are inevitably from another person's viewpoint. I am grateful that they bother to tell me anything at all. Nevertheless, there persists within me at times the scratchy impatience to see for myself all these things once more. The daily, hourly, denial of all this is one of the things that deepens the hurt of blindness.

I know that things must have changed considerably during the span of my blindness. The change which a single year brings may be subtle but the sum of ten years' changes will unquestionably have lost the subtlety—the differences will be marked, distinct. If I could have a look about, I should probably feel as Thoreau felt when he wrote that he "had no idea so much was going on in Heywood's meadow."

It is not enough to be told that hems are higher, that cars are lower, and so forth. I do not envision ankle-length skirts for when my little seamstress turns up my hems she sticks pins in me much above ankle level. Nor do I picture that today's cars have the "hauteur" of the late Queen Mary's famous Daimlers, for when I try to jacknife into one of these new midget gas-savers, I must genuflect almost to the point of toppling in.

To be sure, I often try to imagine what it must look like—this world about me. From reports I know that there is more chrome, more speed, more color, more concrete spread around everywhere, more people going to more places but with less luggage, more new houses with more bedrooms because now there are more children. Such reports, however, give me only a profile and what I long to see is not only the profile of the current world but the full dimension of the here and now.

Even pictures, if I could but see them, would give me something of the "feel" of today. It is only since I cannot see them that I realize how much pictures meant to me, how much in fact they must mean to everybody. For a long while the world has been told that a single picture is better than a thousand words. No description, for example, has brought me really to "see" the expression on Alan Shepard's face when he came down from that first outer-space flight, but it must have been a glowing thing to look upon.

Pictures—pictures—pictures—of individuals, of groups, of gardens and houses and interiors, of familiar and unfamiliar places—pictures in newspapers, in magazines, in the newsreels and in the movies themselves. How I miss them, and how I should love to feast my hungry self on a carload of them. I may be told that the White House now has a young look, that New York's Third Avenue has emerged, chic and bright, from its past of dim antique shops in the shadow of the old El. I may hear that a new and strong spirit is moving old and distant lands, but all these things would mean more to me if—occasionally, just occasionally —I could see photographs to establish their reality. I sometimes wonder how I have managed to live this decade without the boon of pictures.

A tantalizing part of the look-of-today which I miss is the actual physical appearance of the people who now make up my own personal world—people whom I have grown to love and depend upon but whom I have never seen. Conversing with unseen persons is somewhat eerie—downright "spooky" at times. Often, in talking with friends, I wonder—What DO you look like—What is the expression about your eyes, your mouth? Do you make many gestures and are they telling? Are your hands graceful as you apply your lipstick or light your cigarette? And you, monsieur, do you affect a mustache—do you wear glasses? The lifting of an eyebrow, the special turn of the head, the shrug of a shoulder, the sudden appearance of a dimple—all such personal characteristics identify the individual, but for me they no longer exist. They are all wiped away, much as a damp cloth might wipe away from a blackboard interesting or amusing sketches that had been chalked there. All gone.

Often, at parties, I ask fellow guests to describe each other and hilarious results usually follow. Men, in describing the ladies, flounder about trying to be both gallant and exact—women never seem to come up with appropriately masculine adjectives in describing men. At best such descriptions are but sketchy outlines and at first I tried to imagine the full dimensions of coloring, stature and bearing. I discontinued this practice after I discovered I was making too many mistakes in these mental projections. I had, for instance, been envisioning one friend as a blonde with light blue eyes and piquant features, basing this concept on the fact that she has a light airy voice, a delicate manner, an expressed preference for pastel colors. I was astonished and confused when I learned she is a true brunette, with an almost swarthy skin, dark eyes, and blunt although attractive features. Someone, I felt, had switched masks. Today I do not try to "embody" my friends—I am content to enjoy them as personalities. This goes deeper.

As the next item on the inventory's list of losses, I set down the word FREEDOM. To be sure, I still have unlimited freedom of mind and spirit but a great part of my physical freedom is gone. This is an enormous loss because so many parts of me were rooted in freedom—so many activities, so many interests.

No handicapped person has the freedom of the nonhandicapped. Certain it is that a blind person can not know the freedom of those with sight. In his darkness he has always the feeling of being trapped, caged. By comparison, a caged bird is a free creature. He can look about him, observe people and things close at hand or at some distance, he can see his food, can give himself —unattended—considerable exercise by hopping from perch to perch. He lives in the midst of glorious light. None of these things —simple though they be—is possible to the blind person, and he never ceases to miss them.

I miss the freedom to follow my old habit of rising early to walk about my garden at dawn, noting the play of light as the first rays of the sun strike across the scene. Gone now is the delight I used to feel at this mystic hour, at sight of the miniature rainbow tipping each blade of grass—that tiny finial of dew sparkling with the self-same colors as those in the great bow that spans the heavens. At that hour I often recalled the story of Henri Matisse, the great French painter. When asked how he managed, at his advanced age, to produce canvasses of such freshness, he replied,

"I grow artichokes." In explaining this surprising statement, he said, "I grow many artichokes and, every morning I rise at dawn to walk among them and note the effect of the changing light on those artichokes. It is never the same—and this challenges me— freshens and stimulates my imagination, my ability."

No one who has ever walked in a garden at dawn will disagree with the old master.

I miss, too, the feeling of discovery when such a garden walk would disclose the first green shoots of spring—the bulb flowers, the shrubs. Across the calendar, I miss just as keenly the sight— always startling—of the first leaf to show color in the autumn—

something that never fails to strike one with the same sharp suddenness as a bell rung in warning.

In a garden, at daybreak, I was always strongly, but quietly, aware of what Joseph Wood Krutch, in his *Voice of the Desert,* calls The Mystique, but which I, in my simple way, call the sense of the presence of God. To quote Mr. Krutch further, "Whether you call the experience infra-rational or super-rational . . . acute awareness of a natural phenomenon, especially a phenomenon of the living world, is the thing most likely to open the door to that joy we can not analyze." I miss that door—I used it so often.

On of my best loved freedoms was to drive my car, wherever and whenever I chose. Having this freedom snatched from me has been one of the greatest deprivations of blindness. I loved driving, with an enormous passion, even more than most women, I think. To me every moment behind the wheel was adventure, even if it were the most tedious errand. As for the moment when we would "head" the car out at the start of a long trip, my elation was boundless. Actually, I did more than ninety percent of our driving—and why not? I adored driving, my husband loathed it. It is ironic that today he must do one hundred percent of the driving.

While driving, the car and I were one. The feeling goes back, I am sure, to the time when my father set me up on a saddle horse when I was the "wee-est" kind of girl.

"The horse," my father told me, "is but a larger part of you— an extension of yourself, as it were. His legs take the steps instead of your legs taking them, his direction is what you want it to be, and in time he will seem to follow your every inclination, not just your tug on the bridle. You and your mount are one—always remember that."

When I began to drive a car I merely exchanged the bridle for the wheel—the feeling of being one with my car was the same I had felt for my horse. I had such a sense of oneness with my car that I often felt that half of me lived in the garage.

The realization of what blindness would do to this aspect of my freedom, my pleasure, came to me slowly. I knew that little by little a great deal of what my life had been was slipping away from me and that, although I found this painful, it was part of the adjustment I must make. Two incidents, however, served to show me that my companionship with the car was over, finished —axed out of my life forever.

The first impact came one evening when Clyde said, half to himself, "I must attend to renewing my driver's license." I caught my breath. Previously it had always been, "We must see to renewing our driver's licenses." For the first time the thought struck me that my own driver's license could never be renewed —and that that small slip of identification, of permission, would no longer be part of my billfold's contents.

The second blow came on the day when Clyde said, in that casual way which belies what is coming,

"I've just had a good offer for your car. Will you let it go?"

I must have known that something like this would eventually come up but when it was actually put into words I was really shaken. Clyde went on.

"You liked that car better than any we ever owned and you are probably somewhat sentimental about it because it is the last one you drove. That is understandable, but it is just possible that you might be more comfortable if the last reminder of that activity is removed. The offer is a good one and I feel we should accept it."

I was in complete agreement with him—it was the sensible thing to do. But on the rainy, blustery autumn day when he drove the dear thing away, sounding its horn in a final salute as he rounded the corner, I knew the end of something wonderful and bright had come. Groping my way from the garage into the house, I thought of that car as it had looked on the bright spring day when I had driven it away from the dealer's. It had been young and beautiful then—no doubt it had a mature look about it now—but it had been my companion, trusted, loved. Suddenly I felt bereft, devastated.

This experience, too, was part of the regimen of acceptance for, until that car was really out of my possession, off our premises, I think I still had, hidden somewhere in the deep recesses of my being, the feeling, certainly the wish, that I would see again and that one day I would tear away the thick blanket before my eyes, and once more look down the road stretching before me—beckoning, promising.

At the same time that blindness deprived me of the freedom to drive my car at will, it also deprived me of the joy of general travel. A high percentage of pleasure travel is sight-seeing—and how could there be sight-seeing for me who had no sight? The idea of travel, therefore, did not make sense to me. Why should I go to the extra effort, inconvenience, and expense, only to gaze upon the self-same blank wall I look upon at home?

It was frequently suggested that I go to the shore for a stay— my friends maintaining that I would find it so restful—the rhythmic surge of the waves washing along the beach, the salty sea breezes. It is not necessary, they would argue, to "see" the ocean for one to be benefitted by a sojourn at the shore. Their interest in me was genuine but their reasoning was faulty for, if looking at the sea were not an important part of a shore stay, why do all ocean-view rooms in hotels command higher prices than those at the back of the house or on inside courts? Hotel guests do not pay top rates merely to listen to the rhythm of the waves. If the rhythmic splash of water is all that such a trip offers me, I can obtain a satisfactory substitute in the rhythmic splashings of our automatic lawn sprinkler, and I can enjoy this in the familiar comfort of my own home. Those sea breezes, too, can be very fickle, switching suddenly into warm land breezes. No, I argued, there must be more than such things to tempt me forth to travel—must be something really to atone to me for my present inability to feast my eyes on visual delights—something to stimulate the other senses or something to invite my spirit to grow. Such a place is, I found, difficult of discovery.

Without sight, even the mountains which we both loved, now had lost their allure for me, since I could no longer enjoy their breathtaking contours, their ever-changing colors, the drama of light and shadow moving over their crests and down into the valleys. Even those cool mountain breezes, I maintained, were quite adequately compensated for by present day air conditioning. All such were my contentions in the early days of blindness when I shrank in a curious kind of timidity from leaving the security of the familiar to risk the strange, the unknown. Later on, however, when it was suggested that we take a few weeks' motor trip through the North Carolina mountains, my old love for that region and the exciting prospect of revisiting it overcame my reluctance about venturing forth and I had a surprisingly good time. Stopping at a different motel every night produced within me what the Siamese monarch in *The King and I* always referred to as "a puzzlement" for the wall where the dresser stood last night is tonight occupied by the beds, and last night's bed-wall is tonight lined with a baggage rack and a couple of chairs. Goodness knows how the bathroom fixtures are presently disposed about that cubicle. In the midst of these variants, there was one constant—wire coat hangers, wherever encountered, are the same —noisy, wriggly, noncooperative.

I gained new confidence on that trip, and I learned all over again that life is a series of compromises for each evening we asked ourselves, "Shall we have the cool comfort of air conditioning with its attendant roar or shall we listen to the complin song of the thrushes in the warm dusk?" We could not have both.

I learned, too, how stupidly one forgets so many things. I had thought that, without sight, there would be nothing left for me in the mountains. How wrong I was. Something was left—something that, like an old friend, welcomed me back, made me feel at home. It was the smell of the evergreens—in the hot stillness of noon or in the after-sunset chill. As always before, I found both relaxation and stimulation in every pungent whiff.

Encouraged by the pleasure I had had in the mountains, I embarked on other trips, alway bearing in mind that I must not expect the delights that had come from sight but instead must receive pleasure through my other senses and the comments and descriptions of other travelers. It was not easy to do this, especially when I would revisit places I had known when I had sight.

I recall the first time I returned to the locale of a great swamp. Previously I had always enjoyed the spectacle of this vast watery area. Brackish, rank with a heavy green growth, it was the greatest expanse of absolute quietude I had ever gazed upon. The light above it was alway eerie, no matter what the hour, and although the air was clear, there was not even the movement of sparkle. In fact the whole thing was more like a photograph of a scene than the scene itself—it was that "still." I had always said, There is a stillness here to be seen with the eyes—not just noted with the ears. It was such a spot as Dylan Thomas must have envisioned when he wrote, in *Under Milk Wood*, of a place "where gulls come to be lonely." To me, however, there had never been anything of melancholy about the scene—rather, I had always drawn great serenity from the panorama.

When I went back to it, after sight was gone, and stopped midway of the long causeway spanning the immense tract, hoping I might recapture the old hypnotic spell, I could not summon it back. The audible stillness communicated itself—I was wrapped in it—but the visible stillness was gone, lost forever. A small incident, perhaps, but it is indicative of the myriad small losses which make themselves felt throughout the calendar of my life. Every one of them serves to remind me that there can never be a substitute for what I have lost. It is possible to obtain refills for our flashlights, for our ball-point pens, for our cameras, but nowhere can we obtain refills for our eyes. I never try to deceive myself about being a heavy loser.

In connection with losses I am invariably reminded of the old phrase, "More was lost at Mohacz (Mohatch) Field"—a phrase that came out of the overwhelming defeat—almost annihilation —of the Hungarians by the Turks at that Field in the sixteenth century. It was so bitter an experience for the Hungarians that for generations afterward, in speaking of any personal loss—a horse, a sweetheart, a year's crop—they were wont to conclude with a shrug, "But more was lost at Mohacz Field." In thinking of my own bitter loss I would repeat this phrase and try to scale my individual loss against the enormous losses of wars and other calamities, but this was no comfort at all. Mohacz Field lay nearly five hundred years back of today and my loss was here and now, very present.

To rank my losses in the order of their grievousness never occurred to me but among my friends this seemed to be an interesting speculation. "What do you miss most from the realm of sight?" they would ask. I had no answer to that for I missed so much. One day a friend pegged down the matter by asking,

"Suppose that, like the fairy's three wishes for a newborn baby, you might wish for three sight experiences. What would they be?"

After considerable thought, I made my three choices. That was several years ago. Today I think I would make the same choices. Thus it must be that, if I were willing to spend my precious wishes for these three things, they must represent what I most miss. In reviewing these wishes, it gives me a warm feeling to realize that they reflect basic interests of my life—my joy in human companionship, my devotion to an art form that embodies all the arts, and my ardent response to nature.

My first wish would be to see again my husband's face—the look of devotion in his eyes. To be sure, his uninterrupted devotion is confirmed for me in the heaped-up measures of his goodness to me, his constant concern for me. I hear all this in his voice, I feel it in the pressure of his hand, but nothing can substitute for that spark that used to shuttle along our glance. No longer can I catch the answering twinkle at some jointly remembered incident, story, or phrase. Blotted out is that look of affectionate comprehension, of mutual understanding, as we listened to music, or watched a great play, or when we would come upon a scene of spectacular or of simple beauty.

My second wish would be for an evening at the Ballet. If I might summon a performance from the past, my choice unquestionably would be for Diaghilev's premiere presentation of *The Three-Cornered Hat* in London in 1919, of which I have read many glowing accounts. I think no ballet could surpass, or even equal, that performance of the old story of the miller's wife as

141

set to music by de Falla, with scenery designed by Picasso, choreography by Fokine who danced the role of the miller. Inasmuch as I possess no magic carpet to bear me back in time, I would be more than content to have an evening with any of the great companies of today—American or European—for I know they would have topflight soloists, corps, and direction. Furthermore I would not be fussy about the make-up of the program, although I have, very definitely, my favorites in the wide range of ballet repertory.

To walk again into the theater on the night of a ballet performance, realizing that in a mere matter of moments I am to be whisked into another world—into several other worlds, in fact —would set my heart to spinning. At the music's first pronouncement, I would move into the ballet world of love and hate, tenderness and cruelty, pomp and pathos, intrigue and fidelity. I would lose myself in the meaningful color, the subtle innuendos, the tempestuous abandon—in the languid grace, the staccato vivacity, while the pulsating rhythms surge, die away, swell again. At the end, when the house lights would go up, I would rise numbly from my seat—weary, spent, voided then of all emotion—and go, mute, detached, out into the sharp air of so-called reality.

For my third wish I should choose two magic moments in nature—dusk and dawn.

I should like to look again upon New York in the gathering dusk of a cold winter day, when the overcast sky has brought darkness early and lights blaze from thousands of windows in skyscraper office buildings, in the high towers of the great hotels and apartment houses. With this brilliance spangling the blue dusk, I would watch, spellbound, the whole enchanted scene disappear behind the white and feathery curtain of a softly falling snow. I have witnessed this miracle a few times—I wish I might see it just once more.

For the other magic moment I should choose to be in a certain hill country, to watch again another miracle—summer dawn, moving across the landscape and to see again, as my father used to read to me from his worn old Shakespeare, "jocund day stand tip-toe on the misty mountain top."

To experience the fulfillment of these three wishes would not send me wailing, like Eurydice, back into the dark. Rather, it would renew and inspirit me, much as an oasis refreshes a desert traveler.

I know what I have lost and I know, too, that if I might have full sight back again, I would give a great deal—A GREAT DEAL—but, and mark this, not everything, for if in exchange for sight I should be obliged to surrender those "substantials" of the spirit which blindness has brought me, I might be quite reluctant to make the trade. I will not say that I am supremely happy in this blind state but I must say—and truthfully—that I am not unhappy. Far from it.

As I proceeded with the list—large losses, lesser losses, all of them painful—I fell to wondering, Is there nothing of consequence left to me? I began to explore, seeking to find items to set down on the other side of the balance sheet. I found them—and in plenty. I found them in such abundance that I was given new heart, new zeal. In fact, such a feeling of resurgence welled up within me that I was impelled to set down my feeling in meter. This constituted a novel experience, a stupendous task, for one who had done nothing of this sort since the rhyming days at school. The effort evolved into a sonnet and I entered the painfully born poem in a contest sponsored by the American Pen Women. Authors' names were in sealed envelopes, opened after the judging. I was deliriously happy when mine won first place. The prize money, like most poetry prize money, might have been termed a "potboiler" but at least it was not a Pot Holder.

A short time later the poem was republished in *Performance*, the official magazine of the President's Committee on the Employment of the Physically Handicapped. Through the widespread circulation of this publication, the poem was read by thousands of persons in need of a lift. Thus, out of my effort, came the knowledge—of no small satisfaction to me—that I had something left, something to communicate, to share, to give.

Here is that poem—a Sonnet in the old Petrarchan mode.

SPRING TO THE BLIND

I miss the star world Summer nights can bring,
And Autumn's red-gold pomp, its brooding haze,
The purple-shadowed snows of Winter days,
But, oh, the baby freshness of the Spring.
A bird's sweet grace atilt his willow swing,
A tulip rainbow, dawn-tipped lilac sprays,
And wedding wreath that like a fountain plays.
How can I miss all these, dear Lord, and sing?

And yet!—I still can breathe the fragrant spell
Of wood smoke or a new-plowed field. I hear
A thrush, upon the dusk, a cadence fling.
I trace Spring's pattern in the jonquil's bell
And savor deep the gift of waters clear.
Four senses still perceive Thee, Lord,—I sing!

CHAPTER 9

Traveler's Rest (Continued)

IN the early days of blindness I could not have believed that there might be compensations of any kind in this darkness but as I proceeded with the accounting of my predicament, my inventory, I found infinitely more compensations than I had imagined existed. I was not wholly "in the red," that was certain. I had lost, had had taken away from me, a host of things through this debacle of blindness, but as I pursued, with merciless honesty, the compiling of the Gains list, I noted that a great many things had moved into my life as replacements, as substitutes, for those lost. I noted, too, a difference in the character of the two listings—the losses, almost without exception, being physical deprivations, whereas the gains which have evolved from the blind condition are almost entirely of the spirit, of the mind, of the emotions.

Strangely enough, at the top of the Gains column I set down the very same word which I set down at the head of the Losses list—the one word, LIGHT. This light, though, is different from that light which I lost when my eyesight was taken from me. The light I deal with now is the ever-brightening inner light of which I had been conscious ever since I crossed the frontier of this new land—a light which might better be termed "illumination." Here was a counterbalance to the loss of physical sight. This light sends its beams into the deep places of the spirit, penetrates, the secret spots, thus enabling me to gaze—with awe— upon what Martha Graham, the great dancer, once called the "inner landscape."

As this illumination suffused itself throughout each day I came to realize how it was transforming everything. The expressions of wisdom, of philosophy and counsel which I had loved and depended upon for years now assumed a new glow—the affectionate sympathy between human beings became more shining—all human endeavor, its strivings, its reachings-out, became invested with a brighter radiance. As time went on I learned to "listen to the light." Adults find this phrase difficult to understand but children comprehend it at once when I say it to them. This is because their approach is simple, and this is a simple concept. I also noted that just as most of my losses stem from the prime loss—physical light—so most of my gains come from this new illumination.

One day, for instance, this illumination, this light of greater understanding, revealed to me the dazzling beauty of "simplicity." At once I realized that that great quality had been woefully lacking in my life, my affairs, and I realized further that it was something I wanted and needed. Examining my life, I found that it, like the lives of most persons about me, had become one

146

of multiplicity rather than simplicity—that, in fact, it was filled with what I can describe only by the word "clutter." I set to work to simplify it.

My house had always been filled with "objects"—whether *objets d'art* or not is arguable—objects inherited from parents and grandparents, a few from great grandparents. I had always enjoyed having them about me. Every time I passed through a room containing any of these things I had been given a lift of spirit, not only by their beauty but by their association of sentiment as well. I had never begrudged the time and effort required to dust them, a chore I never trusted to another. After blindness, however, what could many of these things mean to me, since it was primarily the sight of them that made them so dear. I have kept the larger pieces but the smaller pieces and the bric-a-brac have been passed on to other members of the family. This is a continuing process and I have not entirely achieved my ideal—a house of oriental simplicity—in the arrangement of furniture, of pictures and ornaments, of flowers.

Indeed, flower arrangement had become a Vexatious Topicke in our household, for my own fumbling efforts to achieve effective arrangements—desperate though these efforts were and probably because they were so desperate—ended in failure every time. My material would soar too high, sprawl too wide, droop too low. The result must have resembled a cross between a Hottentot coiffure and a walrus' mustache. My husband's feelings about "Arrangements" was that when a vase or bowl was stuffed tight with stems, it was then an accomplished bouquet. Mazie's contribution to the solution of the problem was to thrust a single spike of Prince's Feather into a highball glass, set it on the window sill, then go back to her cleaning. Her idea had the merit of simplicity and, whether she knew it or not, coincided with that of Oscar

147

Wilde who advocated "a single blossom against a background of nothing at all."

Convinced that we could never produce satisfactory results, we compromised—no, we surrendered. We adopted potted plants. As time went on, these came to include five large palms. These flourishing plants are a continual reminder of the proverbial camel, his nose at the entrance to the tent. These palms entered our life as Miniatures of their species adorning the top of some book shelves but they have grown with such vigor that now, after successive repottings they occupy twelve-inch pots and have grown to incredible height and breadth. If this continues we shall be crowded out of the "tent."

Potted plants also afford, aside from flowering shrubs, the main feature of our garden. These can be moved about at will to provide a patch of color wherever desired, to produce a different effect at different seasons, but all the while preserving the essential simplicity of the garden. Moreover, keeping these pots weeded—something which even I can do—is a simple matter compared with the weeding of beds of flowers. In many such ways I strive to attain simplicity. Our entertaining, for example, has been simplified—anything complicated has been abandoned, no matter how much it may have meant to us heretofore.

When I went further and came to the consideration of my general activities, I was doubly appalled by the clutter. Even before blindness I had begun to suspect that many of these things no longer meant much to me but now I was sure of it. It was no wonder that I tired easily at the mere thought of the many things I was committed to doing. Then and there I instituted a new program of simplification. With the sharp scalpel of decision and the tweezers of perseverance I have cut away and drawn out from my life and living everything that has no real bearing on my existence as a blind woman. Today I keep on my calendar only those affiliations in which I am vitally interested. My enthusiasm is confined to these few channels and thus can run deeper. I have pruned my correspondence list, my Christmas card list—I have been almost ruthless in clearing out desks and cupboards and storage closets. I believe it is a kind of inertia rather than thrift that prompts us to say, "I'll keep this—it may come in handy some time." It seldom does, as most of us know. Simplification of this sort takes courage. It also requires reevaluation in every area of one's life. To replace meaningless multiplicity with meaningful simplicity is a richly rewarding adventure. I know. Today my life is as free and clean and brisk as a March wind.

The new illumination revealed further compensations—my dreams, for instance. For years I had regarded dreams as intruders, as thieves of my time of sleep. They never seemed to make much sense when I awoke, but since blindness, they are more than an experience, an interlude, brief and fleeting. They are now a domain—I really want to use the word "demesne" here—a happy domain, for in my dreams I am never blind. I move about in a remembered world. I often compare my good luck in this regard with the plight of the poor fellow in the old Pushkin story on which Moussorgsky based his opera, *Boris Godounov*. This unfortunate man had been born blind and so had no recollection of color, form or movement to rise to the surface. As he describes his lot:

"From childhood I have been blind and know not night nor day. In my dreams, no outline I perceive, nor shapes, but only sounds and voices."

In my own dreams I have many freedoms restored—I move about unaccompanied in houses, along streets. I seem almost to have wings on my heels. I look upon people and buildings and trees and oceans, and I recognize them as such. All this is exciting but the transport of joy is that I always dream in color—glorious, vibrant, stimulating color. It seems to have more meaning for me now than it ever had before—my response to it is livelier. I no longer wish for dreamless sleep—indeed, I wish I might dream the whole night through. My friends in psychology tell me that my subconscious has not yet become apprised of the fact of my blindness and so continues to send up images from the sighted life but that the time may come when, if present conditions crowd in, these colorful dreams may cease. I hope that time is far, far off.

Relative to dreams, I have often asked bilingual persons which language they use in their dreams—seeking thus to discover or establish which is their true *première langue*. Not one has ever been able to tell me. Neither can I tell which is my true life—the free life of my dreaming or the circumscribed daytime life of darkness.

Another item I can set down on the Gains, or compensation, side of the inventory is a growing Objectivity within myself—a condition born out of the blindness.

We blind, I often think, move about in the world of the sighted much as travelers in sedan chairs must have moved, part of the crowds about them but—with the little curtains drawn—somewhat detached, removed, even a bit aloof. A sedan chair life is different from the life around it by just that much. This small aloofness, this tiny bit of removal, is an additional quality, an integral part, of my present life. By the very nature of blindness I am withdrawn, apart, just enough in fact to make me more objective in my thinking, my attitudes, my assessment of people and situations. Such objectivity was more difficult when I could see people, see their disarming smiles, their impeccable dress, the impressive backdrop of their lives. Today I am liberated from the force of such matters. Now I can whittle an individual down to essentials—can "see" him as he really is, and sometimes, I regret to say, he is not so pretty.

This enviable vantage point of greater objectivity does two things for me—it enables me to make cooler appraisals of myself and others, and it engenders within me a more understanding, a warmer attitude toward people and ideas. Such an objective station tends to raise me above most petty considerations—they assume now their true small scale when looked at from here. Thus, to "sit above the floods and tides" tends to produce fairer and less hurried judgments. To a great degree I have come to see the futility and absurdity of tilting at windmills.

All this should not be mistaken for a laissez faire approach. On the contrary, I often know, after such objective consideration, that the thing to do is to "get in there and pitch"—and with right high fervor, too.

The next listing I set down on the Gains side of the inventory was the word Awareness. One word cannot, however encompass what this quality—this virtue, if you will—has come to mean to me. By the grace of the new illumination I have come into an awareness of the innumerable facets of my own life and of life in general—both physical and spiritual. I am more keenly aware of my neighbor's stature, of his almost heroic struggle at times— and I have grown overwhelmingly aware of the many opportunities within my reach in this new way of living. This unfolding awareness is unquestionably one of the most munificent gifts Providence has ever bestowed upon me.

Without awareness we would be a wooden people—with it we are touched with something like divine fire. There is about awareness a mercurial quality that oftentimes makes it difficult of capture. It can be as elusive as a will-o'-the-wisp. Sometimes we have a glowing certainty of its presence. Again, it will draw away, vanish completely. To make this priceless quality our own —really to possess it—we must treat even its most timid appearance with respect. We should never snub an awareness. Instead, we should invite it to become part of ourselves.

Furthermore, to express our delight in its presence within us is important, for expression, outspoken and sincere, is a vital part of the experience of awareness. Too, to be tardy in our awareness or in our expressed acknowledgement of it, often is to miss it entirely.

Have you ever heard someone, in recalling a period or incident, say ruefully,

"I was very happy then—but I did not realize it."

Here awareness came too late. As the reverse of this I shall never forget—no, let me put it the other way round—I shall always remember the look of pure joy that lighted up the face of a certain young woman as she sat talking with a group of friends.

"Do you know," she said wonderingly, as if she had only at that moment made the discovery, "I am a really happy person."

Like the all-round light on a Cezanne apple, her reflected joy shone on the faces of those about her. Here was awareness both felt and expressed.

With me, awareness developed along two lines—that of spiritual values and that having to do with my physical senses—the four that were left to me.

Frequently I hear it said that with the loss of one sense, the other senses become keener. I think this may be true only because from that point the remaining senses are exercised more and thus become more efficient, more dependable. My needs, up to the coming of blindness, had been met by five senses—after that the work had to be done by only four. Therefore, this crew had to work overtime trying to make up the difference. Since my eyesight had been doing more than one-fifth of my sense reporting —I hesitate to estimate the percentage but it was high, very high—this constituted an enormous "up" for the others now. Their initial response was not what might be termed immediate nor altogether skilled. Realizing the sharp necessity of the situation, I pressed them harder and little by little they have come to give me not only aid and support but—further—delight.

I have already alluded to the help my sense of TOUCH has been to me since the start of this handicapped existence—how it enables me to identify clothing, to explore the appointments of my place at table, to do many household tasks. Increasingly, it brings what I can describe only as "sparkle" into every day. Tactile perception can be developed until it is an exquisite possession. My sense of touch frequently needles me into a recollection of color or light, brief though it may be, producing a shining moment in the dark world of contracted dimensions into which I have been pushed.

I am always able to summon a sharp recollection of the play of light and color when I touch my glass lamps. These are a pair, made from old Sandwich glass covered compotes and are one of my finest treasures, not only because of their beauty which charms everybody who sees them, but also for the fun I had in finding them. They are of the moon-and-star design. Although one of my best friends has often dubbed me a vandal for having had them converted from mere antique ornaments into something useful, I have never felt any guilt about it. I make it a practice to spend a few moments every now and again in passing the palms of my hands about the bowls of these old pieces but I trace with my fingertips the sharply incised stars, the plump, cushiony moons and, at once, there flashes before my mind's eye a clear remembrance of how these very surfaces once reflected— and still do for others—the prismatic colors, whether from the day's light or from the light of the lamp itself after dark. There are twelve large moons and stars on the upper part, twelve small ones on the base. I have the absurd habit of counting them. Is this because I fear that since the last count some of these celestial bodies may have spun into orbit in outer space and so be lost to me? Happily, they seem content to remain fixed constellations under our roof.

This method of seeing objects through my fingertips sometimes has its embarrassing moments. People often offer me objects to feel—some article they especially treasure, something they feel they cannot adequately describe to me. I am always delighted thus to share their cherished possessions. All too often, however, these objects are shockingly dirty, but I am supposed to run my fingers along every curve and edge, into every dusty crevice. In the beginning I used to wipe the grime from my fingers at once but, since this always produced such confusion, such apology, I have learned to wait and wipe my fingers under cover of later conversation.

One day while I was being entertained in her home, a gracious hostess placed in my hands a large porcelain parrot and I knew from her description and his bold proportions that he must be very beautiful, very colorful. The poor fellow, alas, was covered with a film of oily grit which was most disagreeable to the touch as I ran my fingers over him. This condition seemed inconsistent with her avowal that he was her dearest treasure. He may have been but that day "Treasure" certainly needed a bath.

I had the reverse of this experience in another house. This was a first visit and the hostess had invited me on the spur of the moment to go home with her and have a cup of tea. I mention this only to show that she had had no opportunity to make any special preparation for me. When she put into my hands a cachepot of faïence and informed me that it was one of her most prized possessions I believed her, for the piece was immaculately clean. Thus, even before she could describe the color and design, I had learned that hers was a nature that cherished what it had.

My sense of TASTE has never been of that ultradiscriminating type that can identify the several ingredients of a dish—a soup, a casserole, a dessert. My palate has been purely for pleasure and not for critical analysis. I relish good food and it has been my privilege to savor some of the best in my own country and in foreign lands. Even without eyesight I continue to enjoy it, but I will not deny that I often yearn for the robust look of a good steak, its surface freckled with coarsely ground black pepper, the rosy plumpness of shrimp, even the placid expression on a head of cauliflower.

Gradually I became aware that, in addition to giving me pleasure, my sense of taste was serving me in another, an unexpected way. Like my sense of touch, it was prodding me into a recollection of color. I had been more or less unaware of the fact that I was fast losing my remembrance of color—that it was seeping out of my consciousness—when suddenly the blessed sense of taste began to bring it back. Noting this I pressed it to advantage and soon I was reestablishing—and quite vividly—color as it appears in food. With very little effort I could enjoy the jewel tone of wild-strawberry jam on the breakfast table, the regal purple of eggplant, the daffodil yellow of scrambled eggs. It became an exciting game and although my imagination continues flabby about a few things, I have, in the main, recaptured the crisp stimulation of color.

My sense of SMELL was ever a pure delight to me but since blindness it has extended itself to become much more than that. Today it atones to me for much that I lost when sight left me. Moreover, it has proved to be of inestimable help in my adjustment to present necessities.

More than touch, more than taste, the sense of smell can bring up color for me and since I miss color so grievously, it may readily be understood how I lean on scent for consolation. Sometimes I walk into our linen closet and bury my nose in the stack of sheets and towels, dried in the sun and wind, and—inhaling deep —try to picture "white," for white is gone for me just as much as pink or yellow or green.

The great impact which scents have upon the emotions is generally recognized—by association they can transport us many miles, many years, can change our mood. In addition to the pleasure it gives me my sense of smell is of practical assistance to me, for it is a very sharp reporter, stimulating me to project my surroundings quickly and surely. The smell of lumber and fresh plaster, as I pass by a new building brings up the picture faster than the sound of hammers or the click of bricks being laid up. I find my sense of smell also brings me excitement, anticipation. There is, for instance, excitement in the smell of rain that runs before a storm, the smell of books in a great library as I anticipate that somewhere among them is the one I am looking for, shall surely find. I have a keen feeling of anticipation when I go to visit in a house that has the smell of soap-and-water cleanliness and of beeswax furniture polish. I am certain that I shall find some point of congeniality with the mistress of that home.

It is when we come to the consideration of the perfume of flowers and fruits, of the bouquet of a fine wine, that my sense of smell goes more than a little dizzy. Today, flowers mainly mean fragrance to me. In my sighted days, fragrance, I believe, came second to my delight in the form and color of flowers. Now I am intoxicated, almost awed, by the various perfumes I breathe—such shades of scent there are—such nuances of fragrance. There is a chromatic quality about it, the gradations are that fine. I am a better judge of fragrance now that I am not influenced by the superb form of petal nor by a well-nigh indescribable hue.

Many of my finest and happiest hours are those I spend on our screened porch—architecturally unique in that it is open to the four points of the compass. Here, as season follows season, I can be one with the fragrance of roses and lilies, of gardenias and honeysuckle, jasmine, orange blossoms, and tuberoses. The splendid flowering of camellias, of azaleas and hibiscus are lost to me since they lack fragrance, but if their perfume were in proportion to their beauty, as I remember it, I think I could not bear up under it. Then, too, there is the paler fragrance of the petunias, and the pervasive cloud of sweetness from the loquat, that slightly mad tree which blossoms in the fall and fruits in the spring. We have no magnolia tree in our own garden but sometimes, from the nearby woods, there drifts to us the overpoweringly heavy perfume of magnolia blossoms, something which instantly conjures up for me the exact look of white.

In addition to the perfume of flowers, my recollection of color is activated by the smell of fruit—melons, oranges and lemons, peaches, even pears, that queen of fruits. And to walk through the fragrance of an apple orchard in full fruit, or through a vineyard at the time of grape harvest, is to tread at least the vestibule of heaven.

Paradoxically, these exciting perfumes tend to create within me a calm content which is the specific I need for the feverish yearning to see again my beloved New York—to see the high, heathered hills of Scotland, the old and mellowed towns of Umbria, and Rio's harbor, with that solitary figure looking down upon it. Along with "the moonlit gardens of the Moguls," all these have slipped into a limbo of voluntary relinquishment, and in their stead I accept this quiet, scented garden.

Perhaps some day I shall realize my dream of years and acquire a small aromatic herb garden—not on such a scale as the one in Brooklyn's Botanic Gardens where, I have been told, blind persons may feel, smell, even taste, the leaves of various herbs. I cherish the recollection of the herb garden at The Cloisters in New York, high above the Hudson. Whenever I visited The Cloisters I went first to pay my respects to those glories, the Unicorn Tapestries, then at once to the herb garden. Its position on the south side of the great medieval structure made of it a kind of suntrap and the fragrance of the herbs was thus intensified. This redolence was a perfect complement to the arched setting, to the mood of tranquillity.

The sense of HEARING, for most people, stands next to eyesight in importance. My sense of hearing had always been acute, probably due to my years of working at music, but after I was thrown into the dark I began to hear much that I had never been aware of before. Music displayed greater richness, the sounds of nature multiplied for me, human voices told me more. I began to perceive that the sense of hearing was to be of greater and greater importance, not only as a source of pleasure, but as a means of keeping me from danger. One of the hazards of

158

blindness is that of colliding with objects—furniture, doors, the top of an automobile as you enter it. I decided to practice "obstacle perception," which is nothing more than listening for even a faint reflection of sound waves from an object as you pass by it. It is amazing how much information one can gather from this. Proficiency here requires time and close attention but I have found it well worth the effort for it enables me to move about with greater assurance. Obstacle perception is especially helpful in the kitchen where open cupboard doors, like cupboard doors the world over, are apt to give one a nasty bump. When I first began experimenting with this, I thought that by humming I might gauge the distance to an object from the small echoes, but almost at once I discovered that the humming interfered with my hearing, so I abandoned that approach and substituted a brisk hand clap or a single syllable spoken sharply. On an uncarpeted floor I often exaggerate the slapping sound of my shoe sole as I take a step—this produces a fine echo. Such practices provide an engrossing study, of endless interest, and stimulate one to utilize innumerable resources. I have been told of one blind man who, in passing through a densely wooded area every day, safely negotiates his way without a cane merely by snapping his fingers as he moves along and noting how this sound bounces back from the trees.

I use my ears, too, in recognizing my friends. I now identify scores of persons by their voices. I myself do not regard this as anything remarkable—for years I recognized people by eye—why not by ear? My friends, however, seem to feel that this ability is rather singular, and the result is that a kind of game has sprung up among us. They will address me by name, then wait for me to greet them by name. All of us enjoy this and I work hard at it so as not to disappoint them. Once I have established the timbre of someone's voice, along with any individual or distinguishing inflection, I am quite positive ever afterward of that person's identity. Of course if, in a prankish mood, someone disguises his voice, I am baffled much as a sighted person would be in attempting to identify someone wearing a mask. I do not know whether my kind of identification would stand up in a court of law but I have full confidence in it.

In all this I am greatly helped by the fact that I usually meet certain persons in certain places—while shopping, or at Fine Arts meetings, the Little Theater, music events or lectures, the Club, campus band concerts. By associating persons and places I can more readily establish identity. Sometimes, however, I come upon a voice that does not seem to "fit" the immediate surroundings. Then I need a little cushion of time.

Something like this happened recently when I attended the singing of a Bach cantata at a local church. Afterward, as I passed through the vestibule, a hand was laid on mine and a masculine voice said,

"I just want to say 'hello' to you, Mrs. McCoy."

Then, still holding my hand, he was silent. From this I knew he was someone accustomed to playing the guessing game but at the moment there was nothing familiar about the voice. I groped but something was fogging my sense of recognition. Seeking a further clue I asked,

"Ordinarily, would I expect to meet you in a church?"

At once he broke into a gale of laughter, declaring,

"Indeed—you would not."

Then I knew—he is one of the few out-and-out atheists I have ever known. This evening he had come to hear a good friend sing a solo part in the production.

In countless ways my sense of hearing is building a bridge

between the old life of sight and the present life without it. I have, for one thing, come into closer rapport with the birds. Previously, I had, through casual observation and some reading, been only moderately aware of their presence, of their plumage and song. I knew they had disagreeblae traits as well as pleasant and amusing ones—that there are among them thieves, brawlers, even tipplers, when they have the chance. In my present life I have come to know them as fellow creatures and am convinced that their good points far outnumber their bad ones.

I now live in what is a migratory lane for these, the smartest travelers in the world. Long before my friends report that the fields and woods are greening with spring or flaming with autumn, I hear these knowing creatures moving in upon us. I like to sit in my garden and listen to them all about me—fluttering among the branches of the trees, pecking and scrabbling in the grass and leaves, chirping, frequently bursting into snatches of song. Sitting thus I often recall some passages from the writings of Saint Brandon, that intrepid Irishman, who sailed the seas in the sixth century and has left us fascinating and detailed accounts of his voyages. This is the way—in the language and spelling of his time—that he describes some unique birds he chanced upon:

Thereby stode a fayre tree, full of bowes, and on every bowe sate a fayre burde, and they sate so thycke on the tree that unneath ony lefe of the tree myght be seen, the nomber of them was so grete, and they songe so meryly that it was an hevenly noyse to here. And than Saynt Brandon commaunded of one byrde to tell hym the cause why they sate so thycke on the tree, and sange so meryly. And than the byrde sayd, "Somtyme we were aungels in heven, but when

161

our Mayster Lucyfer fell down into hell for his hygh pryde, we fell with hym for our offenses, some hygher, and some lower, after the qualyte of theyr trespace, and bycause our trespace is but lytell, therefore our Lord hath set us here out of all payne in full grete joy and myrth, after His pleasynge, here to serve Him on this tree in the beste manner that we can."

The birds in our trees are, I feel sure, operating under the same commission and "singe full as meryly" as those in this tale and, aside from an occasional tiff among themselves, seem always to be having a gay and exciting time. What is more they pass on this feeling to me and I am given added courage to know that they, too, are, in a way, "going it blind." These feathered tourists never buy maps, never check with some avine AAA to learn which fly-lanes may be impassable or dangerous, never study lists of recommended dining and lodging places, never wire ahead for reservations. They simply set out, trusting to that mysterious little mechanism somewhere within them. Their courage to venture brings me into real kinship with them.

During the short time they stay with us, I am often tempted to emulate the good Francis of Assissi and engage them in conversation. Then one morning they are gone, but another flight takes their place. After a while the full migration comes to an end and I am bereft of their company. But in a few months, back they come, traveling in the opposite direction and I am overjoyed to have them once more. Again they are all over the place and in a great dither, hopping, screaming, raking about in the grass. I like to think that all this is to show their delight in being back in the friendly Assissi climate of our garden, but I sadly suspect they are telling me, in the way humans might, that they had miserable accommodations at their favorite resort this season, that food and service were abominable, and the other guests not in the least congenial. I feel sure they are telling me further that they will never return to that place—and I am almost equally sure that next season will find them back at the very same resort. This is the way of human beings—it may be the birds' way, too.

My acquaintance among the birds is not limited to those who migrate. I have many friends among those who stay year round. They are good company—all of them—those who entertain me during the daylight hours and those that waken me in the night. There is one kind of owl whose eerie cry has so much of the swamp in it that I am invariably reminded of the old song *Chloe*.

There is a mockingbird—I am sure he is a tenor—who regales us with nightlong recitals during the nesting season. His stage is the giant live oak in the middle of our garden. We know that primarily his performance is programmed to entertain his mate sitting on a nearby nest. We concede that those portions of his singing that are tinged with more than a little swaggering blarney are "strictly for the Little Woman," but we like to think that the haughty, emphatic recitatives and the lush liquid cadences are beamed in the direction of our windows. He seems indefatigable in his performance but I am equally indefatigable as a listener. I adore him, and never begrudge the sleep I must lose in order to listen to him.

And then there was Butch—that minim of affection and impishness, wrapped in a handful of blue and green feathers— Butch, who lived his life with gusto and merriment and who came to the end of it in the right way, too—for he made one last splendid flight, then fell at our feet. He who had been so full

163

of life was suddenly emptied of life. Where now was the sweet spirit that had animated that little bundle of gay plumage? How could so real a thing evaporate into nothingness? I had lost the companion of all my blind days.

It was, however, his austerity in death that tore a hole in our hearts.

CHAPTER 10

I Unpack My Luggage

GILBERT K. CHESTERTON once said he hoped to have the time in his later years to unpack the luggage of his life and see what was there. He had collected so much and he wanted to sort it all out and enjoy it. I do not know whether or not Mr. Chesterton ever found the time to do this—I hope he did.

At this point on my journey—I was still enjoying Traveler's Rest—I bethought me of my own luggage. Up to now I had been so occupied with the physical adjustment to my new condition that I had all but forgotten that luggage of the spirit which I had carried with me over the rough road. Now was the time to have a look at it—to unpack, sort, and so learn exactly what I had brought from the old country of sight into this

165

new land—learn how much, if any, of it could be used in my new life. I was astonished at what I found.

It was an accumulation, as most storage is, and although the outside showed some wear and tear, what I began to draw from the various pieces of luggage was fresh and of ageless beauty, for these were the things of spirit, things passed on to me by others, as well as what I myself had collected.

Everyone who has been privileged to explore the contents of old boxes and chests knows the delight that accompanies such adventure. It is usually hard work but it is never a chore for those who love "treasure." One is constantly exclaiming, "Oh, how beautiful—how charming—how quaint," and then "I know the very place I can use this." Excitement grips one as article after article is drawn from the place where it has been waiting so long—waiting to be unwrapped—its beauty to be rediscovered, rejoiced in.

From the great pile of my luggage of the spirit, I chose at random—it was the "gentleman's bag" of the type my father had used for years—a sturdy, pebble-grained leather Gladstone. This bag, a relic of our father's bachelor days always held a peculiar fascination for us children. There was about it a veritable aura of peregrination that excited us. It had gone with him on so many trips, to so many places, "even to Texas," as we habitually concluded our catalog of his jaunts.

From this huge bivalve of the luggage species, I drew out first a well-worn copy of the plays and sonnets of Shakespeare. It was with this volume that my father set my standard for all literature, perhaps for all the arts. My whole life has been lived—literally—within arm's reach of these "compleat works," but even less than arm's reach in my mind, for the long memorized portions which my father required of me are a part of me forever

—closer than breathing. Those lengthy assignments for memorizing used to loom as large as icebergs to me but how I bless him today, for now, in my blindness—and just when I need them most—they rise to the surface of my consciousness and with some bit of wisdom encourage me, set me straight. Sometimes, indeed, they merely "pleasure" me.

I reached again into the Gladstone and brought out, wrapped neat and tidy, my father's insistence on orderliness. It was he who trained me in this virtue—little by little, and more by example than precept. I came to love order almost for order's sake—it assumed the beauty of symmetry. My mother subscribed to the same rule of orderliness—"A place for everything, and everything in its place"—but there was this difference in their interpretation of it. My mother would have "temporary" places for things—"Until the next time I go to the attic," or "Until I can show it to my sister Flora," and so forth. Not so my father. When he had finished with an article—a book, the field glasses, his hatbrush—back it would go to its proper place, and no delay about it. My mother's practice was unquestionably more comfortable but, as time went on, I adopted my father's way. I saw that in the long run it saved time. My mother's "temporary" places would be fatal to me now in blindness. My father's training, on the other hand, is one of my mainstays today. I bless him, for what would my life as a blind person be without my built-in sense of order—without the precise storing, the accurate mental filing of the exact location of my various effects. Without it, indeed, life might be a hotchpotch, not only for myself but, in all likelihood, for everybody whose life touches my own. There were other things in the old Gladstone bag but these were what I could immediately make use of in my new life.

The next piece of luggage that caught my eye was a small

valise of my mother's. I opened it gently, tenderly, for its feminine fittings, even an imagined whiff of Parma violet, were so remindful of her. What I drew out seemed mere whisps of something, as cobwebby as one of her lace-edged handkerchiefs. I looked more closely—I caught my breath. They were a handful of adages.

My mother's family was much given to the use of adages. In all their conversation these succinct small phrases floated about like so many bright colored autumn leaves that drift down to cover the lawn, ankle deep, and one might walk through them, kicking them up in great whirls and so find the most beautiful, the most lovely ones. One might then gather these choice ones into a tight little bunch. As I clutched this imaginary handful, I heard again some of those esteemed and well-loved maxims:

"If a thing is worth doing at all, it is worth doing well."

"Loin des yeux, loin du coeur"—the English equivalent, "Out of sight, out of mind" seemed less poignant.

"Step by step, one can go a long way" or *"Pas à pas, on va bien loin."*

"Über den Sternen ist Ruh"—"Beyond the stars there is rest." This one was often used to prod us when we pleaded weariness.

There was the stern Latin reminder, *"Nihil sine Labore"* and from Holy Writ, "A soft answer turneth away wrath."

Quaint? Perhaps. There were dozens of them and they shuttled from language to language. I still love them and I have used many of them in this book. In all likelihood I shall continue to use them for the rest of my life. I find that, on the whole, they are better directives than singing commercials.

Two of these maxims were special favorites of my mother. I used to think that I had heard the one about doing things well, as many times as there were numbers in the arithmetic book. It still comes back to me whenever I am tempted to be a bit slip-shod about something. It was the *"pas à pas"* precept, however, that my mother used when she wanted to encourage me to per-severe at whatever I was engaged in. I never hear this phrase but that I am carried back to the broad latticed porch that overlooked our garden—a little girl sitting with her mother and being taught the art of needlecraft.

It was there that I learned to "run a fine seam." I started on quilt blocks, as was the custom. Why these things were consid-ered ideal for beginners is still a mystery to me for, in point of fact, they can be done well only by someone quite expert with the needle. The stitches must be tiny, the seams tight but not puckery, and what little girl of eight can achieve such? The seams I produced followed a zigzag course like that of old "snake" rail fences. Naturally, I was then required to rip out the stitches and replace them with better workmanship if, perchance, there was any cloth left after my feverish ripping. Becoming restless with all this, I would protest, as any child might. I would ask plain-tively why I must work so hard on something we never used in our house anyway. Then it was that my mother would bring in the "Step by step." Quilt blocks, it seemed, were the first "step."

So it was that, *"pas à pas,"* I went along—learning to feather-stitch, to blindstitch, to roll-and-whip. Through it all my gentle mother would counsel and encourage me, for she was doing more than just teaching me this stitchery. She was at the same time teaching me precision, symmetry, appreciation of craft, and patience. Above all of them, perhaps, she wanted me to learn pa-tience, for it was an innate part of this lovely creature who was my mother.

I often sat looking at her—just for the pleasure that looking gave me. She was a very pretty woman and there was about her a sweet graciousness that was irresistible. She had always the knack of making everyone appear better than he really was. My father, when describing her, frequently quoted from his favorite Source Book—from *King Lear*, to be exact—"Her voice is ever soft, gentle, and low—an excellent thing in a woman." She moved through life as she moved through her home, her garden —quietly, serenely, and always smiling.

As a young child I was often presented to friends of my mother's youth, including some of her old beaux. Whenever it was one of the latter, he would invariably look at me searchingly, always a bit regretfully, sigh and say,

"Ah—but your mother—she was a radiant blonde, thoughtful of everyone about her. Best of all, she was a good listener."

I knew what was meant. My brothers and I were like our father—we were talkers. Thus, with the ratio of four to one, and the spate of our talk "bank full," she was, perforce, still listening. She tried very hard to make a good listener of me, but long before I had reached my teens she had abandoned that hope.

When she died, it was January and about the open grave on that cold day were great mounds of snow, banked with flowers. As the casket rested there a moment, a curious thing occurred. From nobody knew where, several honey bees appeared and moved slowly from blossom to blossom. Summer bees in midwinter—it was unheard-of. Yet to me it was most fitting—symbolic of the sweetness that had always drawn others to her. In some measure this took away the sting of death.

Pas à pas, she had come to the end of the *bien loin*—moreover, she had "run the race with patience," as the good St. Paul exhorts us. And patience is what the adage really taught and in patience I could honor her. I laid the other adages back in the little valise but I kept the "Step by step." My mother would have been so

170

pleased at my using something of hers, especially something so well-worn.

Almost at once I thought of a place where I could use this virtue, patience—and then of another, and still another—the number was limitless.

I began to use it when people pushed me. These "pushings" are usually the result of an outgoing impulse to help me and, sensible of this, I try to check the natural reaction which is to resent and resist with all my being. The sensation which a blind person experiences upon being pushed is painful, frightening. Moreover, it induces such a sense of incompetence. I am always happy to be led in any direction, but to be pushed is a rudeness I cannot easily shrug off. It is little short of an affront. For example, it is so small a courtesy, so simple a gesture, to place a blind person's hand on the back or arm of a chair, to indicate its location. He can then seat himself as effortlessly, as unobtrusively, as his sighted friends. I recall the way in which one kind but unthinking host grasped me by the elbows and deposited me—really dumped me—into my chair at the dinner table. We had reached the dessert before I felt even moderately recovered from this thoughtless treatment.

Even worse was my experience at a women's luncheon where there was a large crowd and the tables were of necessity placed close together. I could so easily have followed my fellow-guest if she had given me the opportunity but instead, and without warning, she quickly stepped behind me, gripped my elbows and propelled me, willy-nilly, through the maze of tables and chattering women. I felt I must resemble one of those store window manikins being pushed about by the window dresser and I wondered if my arms were likely to be detached or if my hair, like a wig, might at any moment be snatched off until needed. It was, to say the least, an undignified entrance and although I did not reach a "rolling boil" I confess I simmered with chagrin.

Today I employ patience, too, when people shout at me—and it is amazing how many do this, feeling undoubtedly that because I cannot see I cannot hear. Such shouting serves to erect still another barrier for me—setting me apart from so-called normal persons.

At the other extreme from the shouters are the whisperers. This whispering would be hilariously funny if it were not for the fact that the whisperer erects the highest barricade of all—he not only sets me apart, he erases me completely.

Recently we took a few articles to a jeweler for some small repairs. I explained to the man behind the counter what I wanted done and asked what the charge would be. Instead of answering me directly he began to ask Clyde a number of whispered questions—"Do you think she wants it this way?—Would she like everything cleaned?" and so on. Like the "Blythe Spirit," I was invisible to him but, with my mother's patience prompting me, I eased back into his range of visibility and the conversation.

Another instance of the whisperer occurred in our own home. We had several callers that afternoon and during a lull in the conversation I heard one of the women ask Clyde in a hoarse whisper,

"Would she mind if I smoke?"—the "she" obviously referring to me.

With a chuckle Clyde asked, good-naturedly, "Why don't you ask her? She's still with us."

Everybody laughed and I said, "Certainly you may smoke," and passed her an ash tray. From then on I was counted as among those present.

Patience—patience—patience, and then still more patience. It is both the warp and woof of my life today and I am glad it was part of the luggage I brought with me.

What I drew next from the pile of luggage was my grandmother's reticule—a plump black silk bag, dripping with cut jet fringe. This reticule was part of her calling costume—in it she carried her small folding fan, a little silk coin purse and other oddments. Best of all there was always some exciting treat for each of us children. The old feeling of expectation bubbled within me again at the memory of the reticule—did it hold something for me now? It did—a bit of counsel I had often heard her give—

"When a thing is finished, put a decent end to it, and then never look back."

She had said this over the years to uncounted persons and now she was saying it to me. There was an incisiveness about everything my grandmother said, everything she did. It was like a clean-cut line—no ragged, deckle edges to her thinking, to her actions, to her speech.

Meditating on her counsel, I happened to think of a similar sentiment expressed by J. B. Priestley in *The Good Companions*. The line occurs when the old man, in saying good-bye to the players, exhorts them—

"May ye mak' good companions o' t' fowk as comes to see and hear ye, and may ye niver look back."

My grandmother and Mr. Priestley—a compelling combination.

I began to realize what their terse counsel would mean to me now in practical everyday terms. It would mean, I saw, that I must go farther than mere acceptance of my present situation— I must put away all questioning about my fate—must fight the temptation toward the fierce nostalgia for the sight I once had and the independent life which sight had once afforded me. This would involve a strict regimen but it was what they meant when they said, "Never look back."

I have taken these words literally to heart and I never dredge up nor recount the harrowing days, the clinical details, of the hospital experiences. There is nothing I can say about any of this that would prove helpful to others—such matters are the province of the medical men. My province, and the province of this book, is to hearten the spirit, lift the morale, of persons seeking "a way out" after some personal disaster—whether that disaster be physical, or emotional.

I reached again into the great pile of luggage and came upon a surprise—a faded old bandanna, made into a bag by drawing the corners together and tying them in a tight knot whose ends looked for all the world like tired bunny's ears. As I loosened the knot, out came an admonition—conveyed not in soft gentle tones but shouted in stentorian command—"Use what God gave you."

I recognized the voice—it was our old nurse shouting to us. Her name was Martha Shoemaker but to us children, after the custom of the time and locale, she was always Aunt Martha and we loved her. She was a statuesque woman, the color of anthracite, with big hips and hands and, above all, a big starchy bosom where on occasion we could—and did—"cry it all out." Along with our parents, she was a powerful molder of our lives and what I had just heard was one of her favorite molding instruments. Every day she reminded us that God had given us arms and legs, eyes and ears and strong backs, and that it was our duty to use these and everything else in the right way. I could remember her calling out to my brothers,

"You boys, now—you're always late. I'm getting tired of it. You used to say it was because it took you so long to button your shoes but now you got nice lace-up shoes and you're later than

174

ever. You listen to me—God gave you feet to put shoes on and He gave you hands and fingers to tie up those shoes, and in a hurry, too. Now let me see you use what God gave you." Then, turning to me, she cried,

"And you, girl—you're big enough now to button up your own dresses, and tie your own hair ribbons. God gave you enough brains to look after yourself a little. Now then, all of you—use what God gave you. Do you hear?"

We heard. The malingering stopped.

Today, child psychologists employ different techniques from Aunt Martha's. She did not know about "high firmness command, high and low clarity correction," nor was she ever troubled about our minds acquiring a "permanent dampness factor." Her limited vocabulary did not include terms like "verbal and visual powers." My hope is that modern methods will produce results as long-lasting, as deep-seated and effective as hers. I owe an enormous debt to this imperious black woman. Paraphrasing Juliet I murmured,

"Good nurse, I would that I might bring you some rich gift to show my gratitude for all you passed along to me. In every way I can, I shall indeed strive to use well 'what God gave me'—and He has given me much."

I began to sense the magnitude of my heritage. The recognition of what I owed to all these persons set a spur—sharp and deep—to me. Future explorations into this luggage would, I knew, reveal much more but for the moment I would have a look at my own travel cases which were among the lot.

These cases contained what I myself had collected either through my own efforts or through luck. First of all I came upon my world of music—intact—and disturbed not one whit by the vicissitudes of the journey. Here was my own personal music life

—the strict teaching of the old Leipzig professors, the hours upon hours of isolation at the practice pianos, then the pleased audiences, the flowing dress, the flowers—then back again to the practice pianos. Perhaps it was worth it.

That part has shriveled now to only a small sector of the great panorama that has been my musical experience. This includes my acquaintance with many of the truly "great ones" and attendance, over a wide span of years, at a long procession of concerts and recitals. It was always the purest joy to sit and listen as these superb artists interpreted, translated, for us what some attuned mind had set down no matter how many years ago. They always brought it through fresh and alive, with just enough of their own personality to give it individual color. Today my joy is the knowledge that this flow of music has not stopped, been interrupted, for through recordings, the radio, and frequent concerts I still have full enjoyment of music—the great symphonies, the chamber music, the lieder, even the Opera, for I can recall and so envision its settings, its traditional action.

What is more, the intrinsic meaning of music for me is discerned more clearly now that my eyes are seeled. (S-e-e-l-e-d is the correct spelling for what I wish to convey here.) This great gift of musical perception is more glowing, more penetrating, now than when I had sight. It is one of my clearest, surest "windows on the world."

The next bit of treasure I brought from my travel case was my passion for words. This was something of long standing, and durable as tweed. It probably sprang into being on the day I received the asignment for my first Latin lesson. I was twelve years old and the professor, a Latin scholar with the incongruously un-Latin name of O'Rear, was a martinet. I adored and feared him in about equal proportions.

The assignment was to memorize the First Declension, using the word "rosa." By the time I had mastered those ten case endings, "rosa" was a bit disheveled, much like a favorite doll, but somewhere between nominative singular and ablative plural a spark had been struck. That day I fell in love with words and I have never been out of love since.

What a debt of gratitude I owe to my professor O'Rear—for, although he would accept nothing less than perfection, he managed to infuse warmth and color into every lesson. He built up for me a rich and inexhaustible heritage. In return, I pray that the holy angels sing Latin verses for him every hour, on the hour. I feel sure that, for him, this would be *"Paradise enow."*

Through succeeding years of Latin study and of two modern languages I came into the enchanted field of translation and comparison. Thus I found that through their words I could walk about in the minds of others, even of those long dead. In words there are such nice distinctions of meaning, such tissue-thin shadings of intent, such delicate gauzy nuances, for words are the image of something felt, of something perceptible to the mind.

Dictionaries became some of my favorite books, and my lively interest in them carried over into my blind existence. Today these heavy tomes are like old friends. Although their contents must now be read to me, I continue to respond to the thrill they provide—bits of literature, of art, of history, even of mathematics, if I am pushed that far.

The derivations of words are for me the most exciting feature—how "this" plus "that" produces "the other"—the mating of word with word to achieve that which has something of each yet which is, itself, a separate entity. The lineage of a word—the tracing of its bloodlines, as it were—is more fascinating than any herdbook, any studbook, even a geneological table of human descent. Furthermore, the dovetailing, the meshing, of our own language of today with those from which it is descended is a constantly refreshing, a constantly enriching pursuit.

This love of words, like the love of music, had come through the journey unimpaired—I could continue to enjoy and use both for the rest of my life. Essentially different from these, but just as firmly integrated with my past life, was a third parcel. This one was packed with memory, remembrances—a record on a kind of microfilm of the mind, of my life's red-letter days—and of gray days, too—memory of people and places I have known, of emotions and events through which I have passed. It was a rich mélange, and an especially precious package because so much of it was visually recorded, and my machinery for that kind of recording has broken down. What I have stored here is all of that kind that I shall ever have—color, motion, form, light.

The phenomenon of memory—the mysterious realm of memory—is something that perpetually intrigues me. It plays tricks on all of us, sighted or sightless. Some things etch themselves as if with acid on the plate of our memory—others, although equally loved, have the mystic quality of a Whistler, a Turner. Invariably, along with the print, the frame, is the accompanying emotion, like a sound track, and they are recalled together. It would be impossible, for instance, to confuse the emotion evoked by the sparkling gemlike colors—emerald, turquoise, amethyst—of the waters off the Florida keys with the emotion evoked by the look of Muir Woods, silent, awesome, and growing more so as the thick fog from the Pacific rolls in and muffles even the quiet.

It is my great good fortune that in childhood I was taught to observe, to note, really to see the things about me. Because of this early training I think I was more perceptive than the average person. Because of this, too, my storehouse of memory is filled with treasure. And yet I know now that I missed so much—large things and small—and sometimes I think I regret the small things more than the large.

How could I, for instance, in my sighted days have overlooked the magic pattern of the printed page? In those days the printed page was just a highway to get somewhere, as indeed it must be to most people. Do you who read this realize that every time you read even a paragraph you are receiving a refresher course in spelling, punctuation, even in the look of your alphabetical characters? Such a refresher course is denied us blind.

Often today as I lay my hand timidly, almost reverently, upon a page of print, a sense of mystery hovers about it and I wonder what it looks like. Are the letters slim and graceful, or are they fat and pudgy? Are the serifs delicate or heavy? And how do the commas and dashes point up the thought? I fall to wondering, too, what does a small letter "b" look like—not a great majestic capital "B"—but just a little fellow, a small bourgeois "b," as it were. It is unbelievably elusive.

Again, why is it that I can recall the "pouf" silhouette of the pollarded trees along a certain terrace walk above Lausanne, the asymmetric growth of the giant saguaros in Arizona, yet cannot remember the beautiful and distinguished handwriting of several of my friends—something which I saw frequently and should, it would seem, be indelibly marked on my memory. How is it, moreover, that I am unable to recall the expression on my great grandmother's face in the old portrait I have known and loved since childhood, and yet I recall with painful clarity the horror of a particular jukebox, jumping with red, yellow, and green lights and screaming with raucous violence. The jukebox I saw only once—the companionship of the portrait goes back many years. Why is the jukebox which I loathed etched more deeply in my memory than something I have loved for a long while?

How can these things be, I often ask myself. And yet they are. I seem unable to accept wholly the psychologists' explanations of such phenomena. I recall vividly, too, the way sunshine bounces about in Rockefeller Plaza on a fine spring day, and how the flags there snap in the stiff breeze that bends the bright-colored tulips, and yet find it impossible to summon up a clear recollection of a sunset. This inability was another of those things which puzzled and troubled me until suddenly I realized that sunsets, like cloud formations are not—to use the musician's phrase— "composed" pieces. Instead, they are improvisations—nature's stupendous improvisations. As such, no two are alike. They are, moreover, continuously changing, moving, flowing. They cannot be caught and held except on a painter's canvas or, with a fast shutter, on photographic film. How, then, could anyone memorize anything so constantly in flux? It follows that, to relive a sunset, one must imitate nature and improvise, must keep the image flowing, in form, in color. Today I can "run off" a satisfying sunset at will, even when the sunset hour is rainy.

Tucked away in the pockets of my travel case I find also many of the personal qualities on which I depended in my years of sight —a warm interest in people and the world in which I live, a healthy curiosity about new things as well as a reverence for the old and tried. I found, too, a certain independence of thinking but a teachable mind, and a dogged persistence which never fatigues me. These are wonderful "finds"—I need them and shall use them continually. They add to my feeling of being "my own woman" again.

So much I found that day in the luggage of my life, yet I knew I had barely scratched the surface of what was there. As I con-

180

templated the enormous accumulation I was intrigued by its variety—portmanteaus, duffle bags, coffers, portfolios. All this represented what I had inherited from the past—from the writers, composers, philosophers, artists, and artisans—from that "sweet singer" David, from Marco Polo, from Rodin—from everybody, in fact, who had planted some wisdom, some perception, within me.

Here was more than enough to fill a huge storehouse and, I told myself, that is what it will be for me. Always I shall know that I can go to this storehouse, at any hour of the day or night—and for me it is always night—walk about, select and bring out whatever I need, whatever I wish, for my present use, my present delight. How rich I am—through heritage and my own earnest effort I shall never know spiritual want. And I thought of what St. Augustine says:

"If you have received well, you are that which you have received."

It was an arresting thought. I pondered it a long while in gratitude. Back in the Dark Place I had felt pauperized. I was not aware of any resources on which I might draw, or reserves at hand. Now the illumination into which the journey had brought me showed me that I had limitless resources—all I had needed to do was to search for them. Now, too, I could perceive that I had crossed the border and come into this new land much better equipped than I had realized.

Furthermore, I thought of others who, through change or chance, must come into a land strange and new to them and I hoped they too would take the time to investigate what they have brought in with them. In every one of us there is stored up some reserve, some quality to be inventoried, evaluated. How tedious, how costly and time consuming it would be to have to equip—outfit—one's self completely for such a change.

Yet, surely, no one can come wholly empty-handed or, worse still, empty-hearted, to the border of a new kind of existence. There is the necessity for everyone under such circumstances to look about, explore, to find the hidden treasure, within or without. It is certain to be there somewhere. There is always something immediately usable—something to build upon. It may be something we ourselves—either knowingly or unknowingly—have laid away as reserve, or it may be something that others have bequeathed to us—some discipline, some strength, some saving grace—perhaps even the grace of humor.

As I called a halt to the day's examination of luggage, a sudden revelation came to me. It was this—during all the time I had been exploring the contents of my luggage, I had not been aware of the Black Beast. It was only when I turned again to the physical world of everyday affairs, that I felt his weight, was conscious of his thick paws across my eyes.

CHAPTER 11

A Large Room

WHEN I thus had taken stock of the assets and liabilities of my life, I scrutinized the inventory and wondered how I could put it to use. It was as if, in the quietude of Traveler's Rest, I was poised in some delicate balance of decision, waiting for some directive—which I was sure would come—to incline the scales. It came.

Ever since the typewriter had become a familiar tool, I had been writing innumerable letters to friends, filled not only with news about ourselves but with subjects we had found amusing, informing, or controversial. Now and then, and with more frequency as time—and the letters—went on, my friends suggested that I expand certain parts of my letters into articles or stories and submit them to an editor. At first I felt that these suggestions were merely my friends' affectionate desires to help me fill up my days but, as their insistence grew, I began to take these suggestions seriously. This was about the fifth year of my blindness.

As scores of other beginners have done, I thought of Sir Philip Sidney's advice—"Look into your own heart and write." This phrase has been ridden so long and so hard that it is saddle sore. Yet for me it voices the most practical counsel, for who can write convincingly of anything outside his own experience, his own comprehension?

I polished up a few things and sent them off. They did not sell —but with the returned manuscripts came some suggestions about improving them. I then set to work with real dedication and I have been steadily at it ever since. In the main, it is gruelling work and takes much more time than a sighted person requires. I must wait for everything to be read back to me, then recompose, rewrite—or tear it all up and start over again. It means, too, that I must isolate myself in the study even when I know there is a glorious day going on outside. This is the way with all creative work. Despite all this, I have found content in this routine, this atmosphere, and now, with the gentle—and sometimes not so gentle—shepherding of a wise and understanding agent, I am as likely to find a check as a returned manuscript in my mailbox.

Thus I was led to Occupation—of my time, my energy, my interest. Again I was actively engaged with life, and the whole span of the blind experience was like an interlude between the active life of my sighted years and the present. And suddenly I remembered something that a wise friend had said to me in the earliest days of the blindness.

Clyde and I were spending a weekend in the house in the coun-

try and our nearest neighbors, a man and wife, had walked across
the fields to visit us. After some general conversation, the husband laid a book in my hand.

"Remembering your great love of reading, I brought you a
collection of Max Beerbohm's short stories. I hope you like
Beerbohm."

I was at that time so wrapped in the fog of despair and surrender that I said merely,

"Thank you for your thought of me, but reading, you know,
like the rest of my life is done for."

"How unworthy of you to say a thing like that, Marie." His
voice was as short and stabbing as a rapier's thrust. I had never
before heard this tone or manner from him. He went on in the
same slashing way,

"Why are you regarding this blindness as the termination of
your life—it need be only an interruption, you know."

Dully, through the cotton batting of my apathy and desolation, I groped for what he was trying to communicate to me. He
waited. I sensed that with his piercing, challenging tone he was
trying to rally me—rally me as Roland's horn had rallied the men
at Roncesvalles. I could not but respond to such clear resonance,
even if faintly.

"I'll try to view it your way," I promised.

At that, he picked up the book. "If you like, I will read one of
the stories to you—perhaps that will prime the pump of your
interest."

He began to read but now the edged voice of rebuke was gone.
Now it was the voice of the amiable Oxonian that he is, reading
to a neighbor and friend on a country Sunday afternoon.

What I had called an "interlude" and our friend had termed
an "interruption" were the same thing, and neither—thank

185

Providence—were permanent. (I often wish we pronounced that word as Provide-ance, it would sound more like what it means.)

As often happens, when one remembrance rises to the surface of consciousness, another bobs up in its wake. This happened now. I began to think of something I had laid away a long time ago—something that, like a priceless jewel, I had admired but which heretofore I had not put to use. Now I dug down for it, brought it out, and was awestruck by its beauty. It was in very truth a precious gem, left to us by that expert verbal lapidary, David. Centuries ago he cut, polished, and gave it a permanent setting in Psalms 31:9. It is a phrase of nine one-syllable words— "Thou has set my feet in a large room."

In a vague way I had known its meaning but now it flashed before me with new brilliance and real fire. In essence, this Large Room of the spirit is Opportunity—limitless, exciting Opportunity, and as much of it was mine as I would explore, would use, would share. I was breathless as the true import of this wonderful old phrase sank deeper into my understanding—"THOU HAST SET MY FEET IN A LARGE ROOM."

Today this room is as real to me as any room I have ever known. I recognize that I have the privilege as well as the responsibility of embellishing and beautifying this room of the spirit —of furnishing it forth with treasures from the old life of sight as well as with those I have collected since The Beast came to live with me. Here is a challenge that strongly appeals to me. It offers a twofold opportunity—first, it enables me to develop my inner life and so make more habitable the place where I spend much of my life today. Second, it makes possible for me, through activity and service, to share this Large Room with others—to share whatever I may have collected so that these others may, in their turn, add to the collection, then pass it along.

186

As I set about the furnishing of this room I thought of a statement once made by Elsie deWolfe, that now almost legendary character who is credited, and probably rightly, with having established interior decorating as a profession. She said—and let it be admitted that she was advocating the use of wallpapers at the time—"Plain walls are the refuge of the artistically destitute."

Without question, the walls of my physical existence are permanently blank and dark but, not being emotionally destitute, could I not bring some kind of decoration to the walls of my spiritual life? I believed I could. I believed I could apply what William Blake maintained:

"What I see with my mind's eye is far more precise and distinct than what I observe in the world about me."

And Marc Chagall, whose canvasses express a mystical import, depicting thought and feeling in fantastic ways, once said of his paintings:

"These are the images of emotions, pictures of our subjective life. The inner world is perhaps more real than the visible world."

On the walls of my Large Room, therefore, I shall depict what life seems to offer me now—what life means to me now—how it looks to me from inside. Chagall could set the drawings of his emotions in brilliant color on canvas to be seen and enjoyed by other human eyes, but what I depict can communicate itself to others only by the way it manifests itself in my outer life, in my relations with my fellow men, in what I write.

Someone may ask: Are these abstract paintings? I must answer this with another question: Can there be—really—any other kind for me now? Representational art is part of that other life. Yes, these are abstracts and I should like to show you just one. I call it GRATITUDE. It is a large subject which grows higher and broader and deeper with every day I work on it.

I am grateful to so many people, for so many things. Every day I am helped in some way—not only in large and weighty matters but in small courtesies, impulsive thoughtfulnesses—the waitress who sees my need and fetches me a sharper knife, the young clergyman who steadies the chalice for me, my small neighbor Janice who leads me by the hand, gently but firmly, into the nursery of their home that I may "see" the pretty new baby Carol.

And there is Sherry, direct and almost brusque in manner, who comes with a rush to "show" me her new dress. Taking my hand in her strong little fist, she moves it about much in the fashion of an artist sketching rapidly. She describes the print and points my finger to where "it is red here and blue there and just a speck of yellow over here." Still guiding my hand vigorously, she shows me the ruffles on the wide expanse of the skirt—"big enough to dance in," she declares. After such explicit and livening description, I really do "see" the dress. Then, suddenly, with a great whirl of skirt, she is gone as she came—with a rush.

I am grateful for these children's ready acceptance of my sightlessness. Most children regard my blindness as they regard airplanes and television—part of their contemporary world. There has been only one exception. This was a little girl, polite in other ways, who seemed unable or unwilling to understand my situation. She would stand before me and, in a kind of singsong chant, would repeat again and again, "You can see—of course you can see—your eyes are open—why do you say you can't see—" Try as I might, and did, I could not dissuade her from this. I finally had to tell her that we both would be happier if she did not come to see me any more. This tedious experience, however, set me to wondering if Lewis's *Screwtape Letters* might have more than a little truth in them. It certainly seemed that a particular demon had been sent to bedevil me through that child.

There is another area in this great abstract, Gratitude, which I want to point out—the grateful feeling I have toward those who encourage me in my efforts. Like many persons, I abominate flattery but I thrive on genuine commendation. It is as stimulating as an oldfashioned "tisane." I must admit that I cannot bring myself to regard as real commendation any statement that has tacked on it the qualifying phrase "for a blind woman"—for example, "You walk very briskly and confidently for a blind woman." Or "Your speech, without notes, was just wonderful for a blind woman." That qualifying phrase is the pin stuck into the balloon of my courage, flattening it. If I do a thing well, it would seem that I deserve to be judged on the same basis as others. If I do not do a thing well, it might be kinder not to mention it at all.

In this matter of commendation I owe my greatest gratitude to my husband. Not exactly a dour Scotsman, he yet is not what might be termed "free with the compliment." I think he has seldom remarked upon any of my efforts without the pronouncement, "You can do better." At first this tended to discourage me—I tried so hard, worked so steadily, and his comment always seemed a little on the meager side. However, as I turned it over in my mind, I realized that, in his use of the comparative "better," he was implying that I was already doing "well." Further, he was with this statement expressing great confidence in me. How much more abundant could encouragement and praise be?

I feel an enormous gratitude, too, to the people in the community in which we now live for their attitude toward me and my handicap. No one here has ever known me except as a blind person. All of us are very matter-of-fact about the blindness—no one ever minimizing it, yet no one ever making me uncomfortable by overstressing the subject. That I am a blind woman among many sighted persons is accepted as readily as that some days are cloudy in a procession of many sunny days. Here in this college community I have lost most of my feeling of exile from my fellow men. I receive and give friendship on an equal basis with them. They have swept away the image of blindness and our relations are established at the level of what lies at the core of our being.

I have the distinct feeling that these people stand ready to respond to any appeal for help I might make but that until I ask for such help, they will not intrude. For instance, they respect my desire to work at my typewriter and, since it is known that I have fixed hours for this work, these kind and loyal friends never trespass upon this time, either by calling in person or by telephoning. To me this is heartwarming—they do not downgrade what I am trying to do by reducing it to the level of a hobby.

In the congenial ambiance of this community, therefore, I have put down the roots of my blind existence and they have spread around and my great adventure now lies in what is growing up from these roots—such strong branches from the stout trunk of my content, such lovely arching branches, thickly leaved, and giving me flower and fruit in season. This makes for substantial living and I rejoice in my good fortune in having found such an agreeable milieu—so salubrious an emotional climate.

For some time I had, to a degree, recognized this wonderful atmosphere but this feeling was crystallized for me recently by the visit of two friends, a husband and wife, whom we had not seen since the old New York days. They were motoring to Mexico for a winter's stay and stopped with us for a weekend. Recalling many pleasant times with them, we had looked forward to their visit. When they arrived I could not, of course, gauge how time had dealt with them physically since last we saw them but they had not been in our house an hour before I began to feel that someone from outer space had dropped in. I seemed unable to communicate with these old friends except in some kind of emotional sign language.

In any reunion there is likely to be a certain strangeness, a catching-up on what has happened to one another during the intervening years, but this reunion involved more than the usual bringing up-to-date of our lives. These old friends had known me only as a sighted person, an active person and, apparently, they had built up a fixed image of what blindness had made of me—a helpless, confused woman, passive, out of touch with the world. What was even worse was that they seemed unable to erase this image even though I tried to show them that, except for sight, I was the same as before.

They felt it was not safe for me to go, unaided, as was my wont, from one part of the house to another. Instead, they insisted on piloting me about, each firmly grasping me by an elbow and pushing me masterfully. They were constantly urging me to "take things easy," to let them do everything for me. I felt like a child who, having reached the fifth or sixth grade, had been put back into kindergarten. I became fatigued to the point of exhaustion with all this overprotectiveness, although I knew it stemmed from their real affection for me, their concern, and, yes, their pity.

I fear it was not a happy reunion for any of us. The reason was simple. These good people had not been companion to my struggle for adjustment—they had not experienced with me my development in a different kind of life. I still love them but I must admit that after their departure it was relaxing to return to my new and more matter-of-fact friends.

The overanxious attitude of our old friends, however, deepened my conviction that the greatest service a handicapped person's family and friends can render him is to encourage him to extend himself to the outermost bounds of his ability—even stretch a bit farther than that—and so help to dispel that painful sense of limitation common to all the handicapped.

In addition to such decorations as this abstract, Gratitude, my Large Room is furnished with many other things of the spirit. Loyal friendships are here, like so many sturdy chests and tables, and the many kindneses which people—friends and strangers alike—shower upon me sparkle in the room like crystal garnitures.

The small candle of my Self which I tended throughout the long journey occupies a special niche in the Large Room. It is a sizable taper now and it is my joy as well as my responsibility to continue to tend it daily. Of course, the Beast is here too, but I have made my peace with him. He has taught, and is teaching, me much that I needed to learn. I do not love him but I acknowledge my debt to him.

A remarkable thing about living in this Large Room is that, once I had disposed about me my many possessions, I did not—and do not—find essentials here different from what they had been in the old territory of sight. Love and kindness, wit and forbearance, compassion and devotion—they are all here. The desire for friendship, for laughter, the quick response to the need of another—these I sense as sharply here as I ever sensed them there. It is such qualities of the soul that tend to banish any intrusive thought that this is alien land—that tend to strengthen my feeling of being at home here.

My Large Room of Opportunity received its finest feature—Sharing—on the day that someone turned to me for help with a problem. Since I had never regarded this room as an Ivory Tower, barred to everyone but myself, I experienced real joy and satisfaction when I began to share what I had collected.

I am always touched that these persons have such confidence in my ability to understand and help them to straighten out their tangles. I have tramped the lonely road out of discouragement and despondency and this puts me at a level where I can talk to those who are now somewhere along that road—the road of the troubled. This means most of us, for everyone is handicapped in some way. It may not be the immediately obvious handicap of deafness, of crippling deformity, or of blindness, but most persons, at some time in their life, have laid upon them a burden, whether within or without, which seems insupportable.

When such persons confide in me their difficulty and discouragement, even their extremity, I try to bring them to see that their problem is not the whole of their lives and that if they are to draw any real happiness from life, they must learn to de-emphasize the disability—physical or emotional. Let us, I urge them, never enthrone our problem to the point where it obscures our real self—what we really are at heart. Otherwise we shall soon become that disability and nothing more. Instead of being known as the crippled one, the deaf one, the blind one, how much better to be referred to as Mr. So-and-So, a real individual who just happens to be lame, or deaf, or blind.

I urge them, too, to strive for as complete an adjustment to their problem as is possible. This is a lifelong project for many of us. I am always startled when someone says to me, "You made such a satisfactory adjustment to your difficulty." I am startled because the past tense in this statement is all wrong—adjustment, like Tennyson's well-known brook, goes on forever. Many an individual makes a fine adjustment to the physical disability but

193

stops short of making a comparable emotional adjustment, remaining resentful, self-pitying, asocial. Until, however, all negative attitudes are wiped out, one has not become "the whole man."

Of those who have turned to me the largest percentage is, I believe, of persons struggling with fear—fear of what their handicap, no matter what it is, will do to them in their field of work, in their social relations with their fellow men. Their fear drapes them like a dark shawl. I understand what they are suffering and I always try to point out that what is oppressing them is a twofold fear—fear of the handicap itself, the problem, the loss—and also fear of the emotional torment which usually accompanies these things. I urge them to perceive the difference between the two. They may never be free of the problem itself but they can, if they will, free themselves of the emotional darkness. I often tell them of my own experience for, although my particular problem has been blindness, I also had the emotional conflict. I go on to tell them of how one day when the fear was almost unbearable, I suddenly thought of some lines from Housman's *Shropshire Lad*. As I repeated them, the lines seemed to have little meaning for me but they afforded an agreeable rhythm and I said them over and over again—

> Now hollow fires burn out to black,
> And lights are guttering low;
> Square your shoulders, lift your pack,
> And leave your friends and go.
>
> Oh, never fear, man, nought's to dread,
> Look not left nor right:
> In all the endless road you tread
> There's nothing but the night.

Ah, yes, I said to myself, but that is just the point—this shrouding night of blindness is what is so frightening. Moreover, I know I can never walk out of it. How, then, can I say, "It is only the night?"

Yet constant repetition of the lines brought me to see that what they said was true for, although I could never walk away from The Beast, I could—and did—walk out of the emotional dark which was "the night about me" and walk straight into the break of day.

No matter what may be the special problem of those who turn to me, there is—always, it seems—the additional problem of loneliness in their struggle. "I am so alone in this," they will say to me, "Nobody seems to comprehend my distress." My own terrifying experiences in this area are still so fresh in my remembrance that I cannot pass lightly over such confidences. The longing for human companionship in any trial is universal—and courage of the highest count is required to keep one going alone.

For one thing, most of us dread the unfamiliar, and to start walking down the road and across the valley of some personal catastrophe is a frightening business for anybody. But, as I try to show those who confide to me their loneliness, your opportunity lies in this very element of aloneness. Even if someone else could make the journey for you—and no one can—their doing so would rob you of your unique privilege of personal victory over whatever confronts you. Often I recall for them how, one day when I was spent with this same sense of loneliness, there came to me fragments of a folk song:

> You've got to cross the Lonesome Valley
> And nobody's going to cross it for you—
> You've got to cross it by yourself.

Here, in this simple, grass-roots expression, lies the essence of opportunity—opportunity to experience the presence of the Great Companion. I never labor this point, however, for awareness of the Presence is something we must come into privately—alone.

I am especially sympathetic to inquiries from handicapped persons as to whether they can ever learn to avoid the emotional hurt incident to their condition. It is possible that some of these persons are hypersensitive about their affliction—embarrassed, resentful, frustrated—but I have, in the main, intimate knowledge of what distresses them. I regret that in this area I must own to something less than optimism. As I emphasized in the story of little King Solomon in the violet, there is no way, I believe, to build up a sure, a complete defense, against hurtful reminders of our handicap, especially the sudden unexpected reminder.

One of my friends recently had such an experience. Olive is a beautiful young woman, in her mid-thirties, happily married and the devoted mother of two young sons. Several years ago an attack of polio left her legs paralyzed to such a degree that she must always use a "walker." She has made a remarkable adjustment to this condition and takes an active part in community and social life. She has fine spirit, but every now and again something strikes that turns her sick at heart.

Last winter she and her husband went to Norway for a visit and enjoyed a round of entertaining. Included in this was a house party at a friend's ski lodge. On the first day, Olive went in the lift to the top of the slope and watched the others as, one by one, they "swooshed" off into the realm of sun and snow crystals and elation of spirit. It was beautiful to see but, suddenly, and without warning, an indescribable anguish shook her—an overwhelming yearning—not, especially, to ski, but to have the freedom to ski.

Her bound condition was in such contrast to the free exercise of the others.

As soon as she decently could, she asked to return to the lodge where she fought it out alone. During the rest of the stay she had a gay time, participating in all activities where she was on equal terms with the others, but she never went back to the slope. This lovely woman has overcome many obstacles but she knows she is not impervious to hurt.

Surprise attacks are by no means limited to the so-called handicapped. Persons dealing with other difficult problems also have stabbing reminders, without warning—a sharp recollection of a loved one who has passed away, the remembrance of a happy way of life that is no longer theirs, the awful realization by parents that their children have grown away from them. Any of these can come with sharp suddenness. The possibility of such hurt is an Achilles' tendon—and at some time, in some place, some circumstance or someone will find it and, although the attack may not be fatal as was Achilles', yet the pain will be almost unbearable.

To all who ask how to meet such onslaughts, I can say merely: Arm yourself to the utmost of your ability—and the best armor, unqestionably, is a determined resolve to stand firm while the pain lasts. It is under such pressure that, as Gilbert Highet in his *Talents and Geniuses* puts it, "One becomes a stoic instead of a lunatic."

Permanently handicapped persons are permanently lashed to their condition and this incontrovertible fact must be recognized. It is possible, however, to minimize the percentage of space our problem occupies in our life. Each day we can whittle down the amount of attention we may have been allowing it—then give this small additional attention to the pursuit of something outside ourselves. Obviously, this will vary with individuals but all of them will have need of one thing, perseverance. A prime example of perseverance under stress is cited in a medieval ballad called *Sir Andrew Barton*. In the story of a battle in which Sir Andrew has been badly wounded, we read:

> "Fight on, my man," Sir Andrew sayes,
> "A little Ime hurt, but yett not slaine;
> Ile but lye downe and bleede a wile,
> And then Ile rise and fight againe."

Could anybody abandon a fight after hearing such words?

CHAPTER 12

The View Ahead

AS I begin to think of tomorrow and of what it may hold for me, I cannot but think also of today and yesterday, for today and yesterday are the stout bridges that are bringing me to the edge of tomorrow.

Reflecting upon the course this journey—a very real journey to me—has taken, I am surprised that mercifully I have forgotten much of the hardship and disappointment I endured. The route has seemed to lead across a succession of plateaus—plateaus of effort, of accomplishment. Some of these plateaus were concerned with my physical necessities and activities—others were related to the things of the spirit.

As I approached each plateau, it presented a formidable aspect —bare, dry. But as I explored, spent time and effort to over-

199

come whatever difficulty was there represented, the place began to change. It took on a softer look, put forth buds and blossoms, and I would begin to feel at home. Before long, however, I would sense a kind of restlessness—an urge to move on to another area, another problem, and I would resume my journey. Sometimes the way was rough with stones or deep in sand, was icy cold or blistering hot—sometimes it all but lost itself and became a thorny overgrown path. Eventually it would bring me to the base of another sharp rise and I would pull myself up—hand over hand and painfully—to this next mesa of striving, of activity.

Time after time this has happened, so that today as I review the journey I do not see the bleak and dusty wastes which I always encountered at first—wastes I often planted in doubt, and watered with the tears of weariness and—yes, frequently—tears of vexation. Instead, what I look upon now is a series of flowering expanses that reach right up to the threshold of today. These remind me of nothing so much as the drawings of those incredible Hanging Gardens of ancient Babylon, rising tier on tier. "My heart leaps up" at so pleasant a perspective and at my part in it.

Pleasing as this is, the real excitement for me lies in the view ahead, for many other plateaus range before me. There are more things beckoning than I shall ever have time for, and I am certain that before long the old restlessness will possess me and I shall resume my journey into adventure. My pulse is elevated at the very thought of it. Until that time comes, I shall continue to enjoy the contemplative atmosphere of this hospice, this Traveler's Rest, this Large Room. Life is deliciously full.

Today I know great quietude of heart. This is not a state of relinquishment—a negative thing at best—due to the physical blindness and its attendant deprivations. Nor is this quietude the result of the years I have lived. I sometimes ask myself: Is this greater tolerance, this warmer understanding of people and problems, this deeper love for my fellow beings, something that years usually bring to one? I think not. In fact, I am quite sure that the mere living of years could not bring what this experience of blindness has brought to me. Years, it is true, can bring opportunity but they may not force one to learn as this handicap has forced me to learn—and quickly. Neither—I must add in all honesty—would the blindness alone have done it without the persistent determination on my part to grow in that blindness, that opportunity.

Many blind people today sense this opportunity and are living useful, happy lives. I marvel and rejoice at the various ways in which they achieve fulfillment. They are active and successful as teachers, lawyers, salesmen, workers in industrial plants, civic leaders, and a host of others. For me the realm of activity which opened, through writing, was of the mind, the spirit, the emotions. This is my field of exploration and I am continually amazed at what I dig up in this field.

In this connection I am reminded of a letter I received in the early days of the blindness. It was written by a friend of many years—in fact she and I played together as little girls. After expressing deep regret at what had happened to me, she concluded her letter with a sentence which I shall always cherish:

"Grievous as this experience may prove, I have every confidence in your ability to rise above it for you have always found something beautiful where no one else would think to look."

Granted that I myself would never have chosen this place of darkness in which to look for beauty, yet, once here, I have learned my friend is right—the things I find in this blackness glow and sparkle and gleam and diffuse a singular light such as no human eye can see. Sometimes I think of Mme Curie, that indomitable Polish woman who searched through those masses of pitchblende to come upon a tiny gleam of radium.

The experience of blindness, which at first seemed a narrow and confining cubicle, has proved actually to be the chute which released me into this wonderful world of exploration so that, through the writings of the great philosophers, the findings of modern psychology, and the wise conclusions of sages and saints, I have had revealed to me the really great stature of man in his essential being and the really great capacity he has for unselfish devotion, even for sacrifice. I am not unaware of the fact that in our world there is much on the negative side—too much. There is turmoil, the sense of insecurity, suspicion. Perhaps, as Albert Camus remarks in one of his letters: "The peasants have read too much Proust." Be that as it may, I have come to the conclusion that, in the main, individual man throws his weight on the side of good.

It has been a rugged climb—this journey—and many persons would recoil at such a prospect. I did—but I made the venture and, because I am now in a position to make a fair evaluation of it, I know it has been worthwhile, richly rewarding. I can—and with no little authority and wholeheartedly—commend it to anyone contemplating such a trip.

"Trouble never leaves you where it found you," a wise adage points out, and if we in our turn are wise we will not resent a cataclysm in our life but will choose to recognize in it a potential for good. I now understand that it was only over some such troubled road that I could have been brought out of the Dark Place, a region I rarely give thought to nowadays. I was obliged to return to it for the writing of this book, especially for the writing of Chapter 2 which, for me, might well be titled

"HELL REVISITED." Writing that chapter was a bitter, bleak and desolating experience during which I longed to put my arms about the terrified and confused woman I was in that dark pit, with the Beast for companion and not the slightest intimation that there was a spark in the darkness. I yearned to comfort and console the forlorn creature who was myself then. Suddenly I realized that she is no longer there. That woman—"poor wretch" as Pepys would say—no longer exists. She has, in a way, incandesced into a new being with Light as companion and the solid conviction that the minute spark is deathless.

Despair in the dark had been strong in me only because I myself had given it strength—unknowingly, foolishly. Radiant illumination has come to replace what I once loved so deeply, and lost. I confess that I have had to work hard to give this illumination of the spirit the chance to strengthen, to ray out. In doing this I have learned that one need not waste time and effort in evicting the dark—one needs only to admit and welcome light as the new tenant. It is as simple as that, yet at times the simple is difficult of achievement.

In the first chapter of this book I referred to my faith as a simple one. In this last chapter I iterate that statement. Over the years I have, intermittently, wandered into areas of questioning and doubt, but always I think I knew I was on a leash—the long leash of God's love. Whenever I wandered too far on such vagrant excursions, I would feel the tug of the long leash drawing me back. This cognizance of His protection goes back a long while.

I am indebted to many influences for this firm and solid trust, among them a small book. It was a present to me on my sixteenth birthday. I still have it. Even in those teen-age years I was **drawn** to what the little volume had to say and whenever I could quiet my dancing feet and mute the music that forever sang in my head and heart, I would read snatches from it, briefly and at random. It is a collection of short essays and meditations, originally published in France about the middle of the last century under the title *Paillettes d'Or*. It is filled with repose and confidence and is one of those books of which we say: One can pick it up or lay it down at one's pleasure. Perhaps this is why it has so long claimed my affection. It is calming but not hypnotic—it is reassuring but not narcotic. I still like to have someone read to me from it. Its language, even in translation, has the tempo, the texture, of another world and time, but the substance of what it says is timeless, universal. Here is a verbatim quote from that book, set down because it so simply and so clearly images what has been my firm support on this journey:

Listen to the story of a simple shepherd, given in his own words:—

I forget now who it was that once said to me,

Jean Baptiste, you are very poor?

True, I said.

If you fell ill, your wife and children would be destitute?

True.

And then I felt anxious and uneasy for the rest of the day.

At evensong, wiser thoughts came to me, and I said to myself,

Jean Baptiste, for more than thirty years you have lived in the world, you have never possessed anything, yet you live on, and have been provided each day with nourishment, each night with repose. Of trouble God has never sent you more than your share. Of help, the means have never failed you. To whom do you owe all this?

To God.

Jean Baptiste, be no longer ungrateful, and banish those anxious thoughts, for what could ever induce you to think that the Hand from which you have already received so much, would close against you when you grow old and have greater need of help?

I finished my prayer and felt at peace.